NIKON
D3200

THE EXPANDED GUIDE

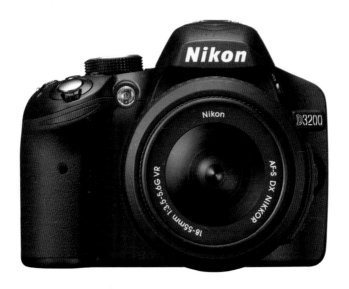

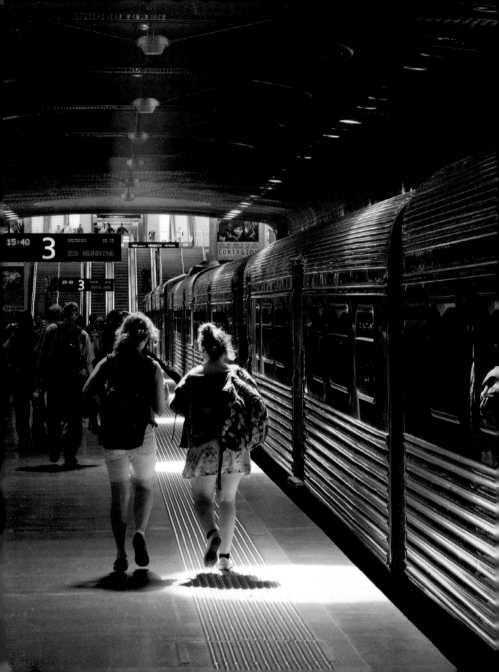

NIKON
D3200

THE EXPANDED GUIDE

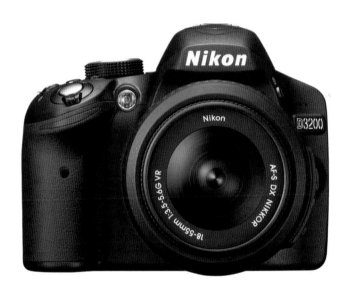

Jon Sparks

AMMONITE
PRESS

First published 2012 by
Ammonite Press
an imprint of AE Publications Ltd
166 High Street, Lewes, East Sussex, BN7 1XU, UK

Text © AE Publications Ltd, 2012
Images © Jon Sparks, 2012 (unless otherwise specified)
© in the Work AE Publications Ltd, 2012

ISBN 978-1-90770-894-7

British Library Cataloging in Publication Data: A catalog
record of this book is available from the British Library.

Editor: Rob Yarham
Series Editor: Richard Wiles
Design: Fineline Studios

Typefaces: Giacomo
Color reproduction by GMC Reprographics
Printed in China

« PAGE 2
Unable to set up a tripod on
a busy platform, I had to
handhold, which meant using
a high ISO setting for this shot.
*65mm, 1/80 sec., f/6.3,
ISO 1600.*

» CONTENTS

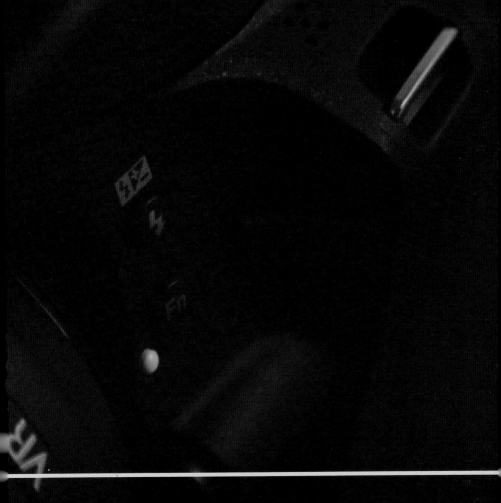

Chapter 1
OVERVIEW

1 OVERVIEW

The D3200 is Nikon's latest entry-level digital single-lens reflex camera (DSLR), designed to marry the versatility and image quality of an SLR with the simplicity and ease of handling of the best digital compacts. It is described as a premium partner to the D3100 rather than a direct replacement. The most noteworthy difference between the two is the D3200's 24-megapixel sensor—the D3100 has 14 megapixels.

The D3200 has a couple of extra control buttons compared to the D3100, but still maintains a straightforward, uncluttered look, as befits a camera aimed mainly at newcomers to digital SLRs. Its Guide menu is designed to lead new users through the picture-taking process.

The D3200's compact size, light weight and relatively simple appearance will make it attractive to new DSLR users, but there's still a powerful camera behind that simple interface, with many features also found on high-end and professional cameras, including fully controllable exposure modes such as Aperture-Priority, Shutter-Priority and Manual.

Crucially, image quality is excellent and—when the camera is used appropriately—meets very demanding standards. It allows, and even invites, the user to explore the wide range of possibilities that lie beyond the basic Guide and Auto settings. The D3200 encourages a smooth progression into more creative approaches to photography.

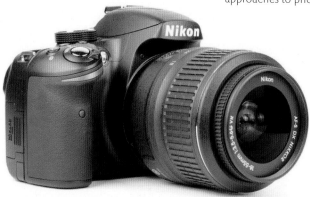

» EVOLUTION OF THE NIKON D3200

Nikon has always valued continuity as well as innovation (although it has shown more of a propensity for radical development in the last couple of years). When the major manufacturers introduced autofocus 35mm cameras in the 1980s, most of them ditched their existing lens mounts, but Nikon stayed true to its tried and tested F-mount system. It's still possible to use many classic Nikon lenses even with the latest digital cameras like the D3200, though some camera functions may be lost—autofocus being the most obvious. Nikon's first digital SLR was the E2s, with a 1.3-megapixel sensor. It had no rear screen and images could only be viewed by connecting to an external device.

The direct line of descent of the D3200 begins with the 2.7-megapixel D1. Launched in 1999, the D1 is the most influential digital camera ever made, and the first digital SLR to rival the flexibility and easy handling of 35mm SLRs. Its sensor adopted the DX format (see next page), subsequently used in every Nikon DSLR until the "full-frame" D3 arrived in 2008. And if 2.7 megapixels sounds mean today, bear in mind it's still more than enough for an HD TV display and almost every conceivable online use.

In 2004, Nikon introduced the 6-megapixel D70, their first "enthusiast" DSLR. The D50 (2005) was essentially a simplified D70, but in 2006 Nikon

Nikon D70 (2004) »
Nikon scored a big hit with the D70, the camera that persuaded a host of enthusiasts and not a few professionals (including the author of this book) to take their first plunge into digital photography.

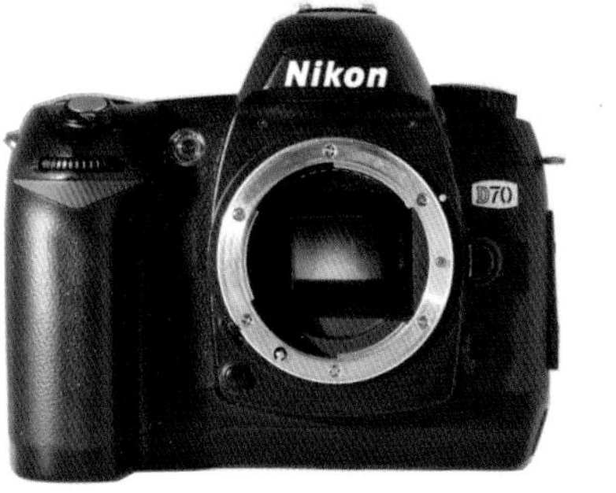

Nikon D40 (2006) »
Nikon's first true entry-level DSLR, the 6-megapixel D40 had a compact, light yet sturdy body and a new, well thought out and highly accessible interface.

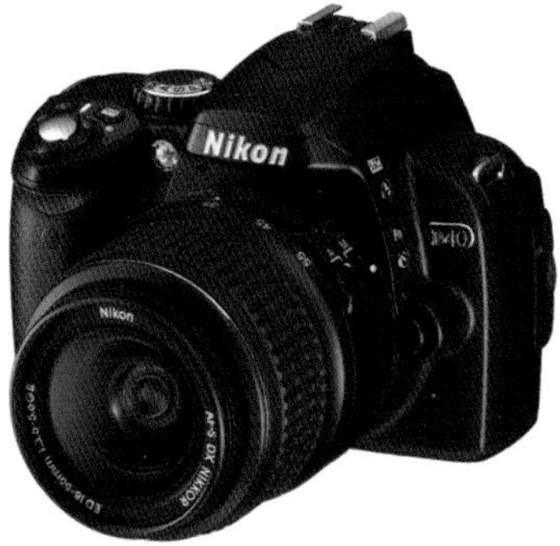

introduced the D40, designed from scratch for ease of use. Its control interface centered on the rear LCD screen, with no separate control panel, and used a single Command Dial where previous models had two. The D60 (2008) added more megapixels but otherwise closely resembled the D40.

Later in 2008, the D90 was awash with new features: Live View, dust removal, better low-light performance and a headline-grabbing movie mode. Many of these were soon replicated on the D5000 (2009), which also boasted an articulating rear screen.

A few months later, the D3000 appeared. Despite the jump from a two-digit to four-digit model number, it was clearly a direct descendant of the D40—D60 line. Though it also absorbed influences from the D5000, it lacked the folding screen, had no Live View and could not shoot movies. It also introduced the new Guide mode.

In 2010, the D3100 appeared. While very similar to the D3000 in many respects, it rectified the lack of Live View and HD movies, and also boasted a new 14.2-megapixel CMOS sensor.

› Nikon DX-format sensors

The DX format sensor, measuring approximately 23.6 x 15.8mm (the D3200's is marginally smaller), was used in every Nikon DSLR from the D1 until the arrival of

Nikon D90 (2008) ⌄
The D90 was awash with new features: Live View, dust removal, better low-light performance and a headline-grabbing movie mode.

Nikon D3000 (2009) ⌄
The D3000 had much in common with the earlier D40 and D60; its headline feature was its innovative Guide mode.

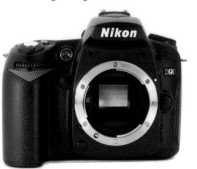

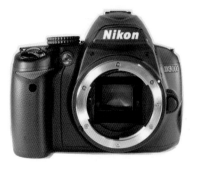

» ABOUT THE NIKON D3200

the "full-frame" (or "FX") format in the D3 (2007). The DX format is still used for the majority of cameras in the range, but the number of pixels squeezed into that tiny area has risen from 2.7 million to 24.2 million in the D3200. The format dictates a 1.5x magnification factor, relative to the same lenses used on 35mm or FX cameras. The D3200 uses a CMOS (Complementary Metal Oxide Semiconductor) sensor with 24.2 million effective pixels, producing images at a native size of 6016 x 4000 pixels, far more than enough for most purposes, and suitable for large prints and book and magazine reproduction.

In front view, the Nikon D3200 is very similar to the D3100; on the rear there's a redesigned Live View button and one extra control button alongside its 3in. LCD screen, and on the top there's a new, dedicated, movie record button. Internally, major features include a 24.2-megapixel CMOS sensor with self-cleaning function, EXPEED 3 image processing, and a maximum shooting rate of 4 frames per second.

Like all Nikon SLRs the D3200 is part of a vast system of lenses, accessories and software. This *Expanded Guide* to the Nikon D3200 will guide you through all aspects of the camera's operation, and its relation to the system as a whole.

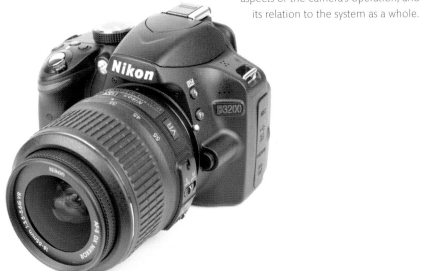

1 » **MAIN FEATURES**

Sensor

24.2 effective megapixel DX-format RGB CMOS sensor measuring 23.2 x 15.4mm and producing maximum image size of 6016 x 4000 pixels; self-cleaning function.

Image processor

EXPEED 3 image processing system featuring 12-bit analog-to-digital (A/D) conversion.

Focus

11-point autofocus system, supported by Nikon Scene Recognition System, which tracks subjects by shape, position and color. Three focus modes: (S) Single-servo AF; (C) Continuous-servo AF; and (M) Manual focus. Auto-selection (AF-A) automatically selects from AF-S and AF-C. Four AF-area modes: Single-point AF; Dynamic-area AF; 3D tracking AF and Auto-area AF. Rapid focus point selection and focus lock.

Exposure

Three metering modes: matrix metering; center-weighted metering; spot metering. 3D Color Matrix Metering II uses a 420-pixel color sensor to analyze data on brightness, color, contrast and subject distance from all areas of the frame. With non-G/D type lenses, standard Color Matrix Metering II is employed. Two full auto modes: Auto; Auto (flash off). Four

user-controlled modes: (P) Programmed auto with flexible program; (A) Aperture-priority auto; (S) Shutter-priority auto; (M) Manual. Six Scene modes: portrait; landscape; child; sports; close-up; night portrait. Guide Mode uses menu screens to guide users to appropriate selection from above modes. ISO range between 100 and 6400, with extension to 12,800. Exposure compensation between −5 Ev and +5 Ev.

Shutter

Shutter speeds from 1/4000 sec. to 30sec., plus B. Maximum frame advance 4fps.

Viewfinder

Pentamirror viewfinder with 95% coverage and 0.8x magnification.

Movie Mode

Continuous feed in Live View mode allows movie capture in .MOV format (MPEG-4 compression) with image size (pixels) of: 640 x 424; 1280 x 720, 1920 x 1080. Up to 60fps capture possible depending on image size and video mode.

Buffer

Buffer capacity allows up to 40 JPEG frames to be captured in a continuous burst at 4fps, approximately 10 RAW files; rate then slows to around 1fps.

Built-in flash

Pop-up flash with Guide Number of 12 (m) or 39 (ft) at ISO 100 supports i-TTL balanced fill-flash for DSLR (when matrix or center-weighted metering is selected) and Standard i-TTL flash for DSLR (when spot metering is selected). Up to eight flash-sync modes (dependent on exposure mode in use): fill-flash; front-curtain sync; slow sync; rear-curtain sync; red-eye reduction; auto slow sync; slow sync with red-eye reduction. Flash compensation from −3 to +1 Ev.

LCD monitor

Fixed 3-inch (76.2-mm), 920,000-dot TFT LCD display with 100% frame coverage.

File formats

The D3200 supports NEF (RAW) (12-bit) and JPEG (Fine/Normal/Basic) file formats.

System back-up

Compatible with more than 60 current and many non-current Nikkor lenses (functionality varies with older lenses); SB-series flashguns; Wireless Remote Control ML-L3; GP-1 GPS unit and many more Nikon system accessories.

Software

Supplied with Nikon Transfer and Nikon View NX2; compatible with Nikon Capture NX2 and many third-party imaging applications.

FRONT OF CAMERA

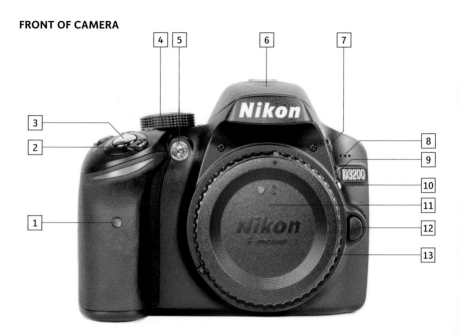

1 Infrared receiver (front)	8 Microphone
2 Power switch	9 Fn button
3 Shutter-release button	10 Mounting mark
4 Mode Dial	11 Mirror
5 AF-assist illuminator/Self-timer/Red-eye reduction lamp	12 Lens release button
	13 Lens mount
6 Built-in flash	
7 Flash/Flash mode/Flash compensation button	

BACK OF CAMERA

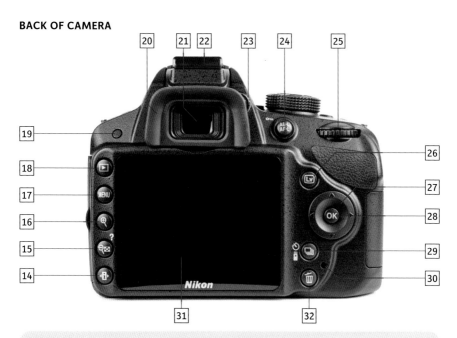

14	Information edit button	24	AE-L/AF-L/Protect button
15	Thumbnail/playback zoom out/Help button	25	Command Dial
16	Playback zoom in button	26	Live View/Movie button
17	MENU button	27	Multi-selector
18	Playback button	28	OK button
19	Infrared receiver (rear)	29	Release mode/Self-timer/Remote control button
20	Eyecup	30	Memory card access lamp
21	Viewfinder eyepiece	31	LCD monitor
22	Accessory hotshoe cover	32	Delete button
23	Diopter adjustment dial		

1 » FULL FEATURES & CAMERA LAYOUT

TOP OF CAMERA

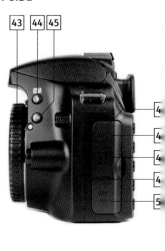

LEFT SIDE

33	Movie-record button
34	Power switch
35	Shutter-release button
36	Exposure compensation/Aperture adjustment/ Flash compensation button
37	Camera strap mount
38	Focal plane mark
39	Speaker
40	Accessory hotshoe
41	Mode Dial
42	INFO button

43	Mounting mark
44	Flash/Flash mode/Flash compensation button
45	Fn button
46	Connector cover
47	External microphone connector
48	USB and AV connector
49	HDMI mini-pin connector
50	Accessory terminal

BOTTOM OF CAMERA

RIGHT SIDE

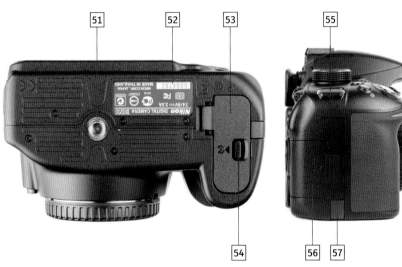

51	Tripod socket (¼in)
52	Camera serial number
53	Battery compartment
54	Battery compartment release lever

55	Camera strap mount
56	Memory card slot cover
57	Power connector cover for optional power connector

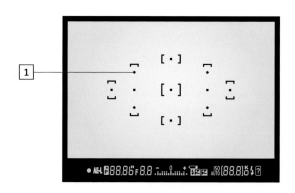

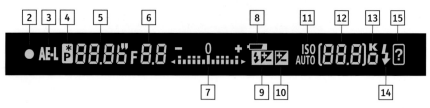

1 Focus points	**10** Exposure compensation indicator
2 Focus indicator	**11** Auto ISO sensitivity indicator
3 AE lock indicator	**12** Number of exposures remaining/
4 Flexible program indicator	Number of exposures remaining in
5 Shutter speed	buffer/white balance recording
6 Aperture	indicator/exposure compensation
7 Exposure indicator/exposure	value/flash compensation value/
compensation display/electronic	ISO sensitivity
rangefinder	**13** K (when over 1,000 exposures remain)
8 Battery indicator	**14** Flash-ready indicator
9 Flash compensation indicator	**15** Warning indicator

» LCD CONTROL PANEL

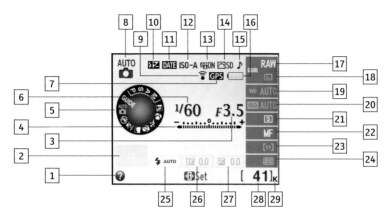

1	Help icon	**15**	Beep indicator
2	Auto-area AF/3D-tracking/focus point indicator	**16**	Battery indicator
3	Aperture (f-number)	**17**	Image quality
4	Exposure/exposure compensation indicator	**18**	Image size
5	Mode Dial indicator	**19**	White balance
6	Shutter speed	**20**	ISO sensitivity
7	GPS connection indicator	**21**	Release mode
8	Shooting mode	**22**	Focus mode
9	Eye-Fi connection indicator	**23**	AF-area mode
10	Manual flash/flash compensation indicator for optional flash units	**24**	Metering
11	Print date indicator	**25**	Flash mode
12	Auto ISO sensitivity indicator	**26**	Flash compensation indicator
13	Active D-Lighting	**27**	Exposure compensation indicator
14	Picture Control	**28**	No. of exposures remaining/WB recording indicator
		29	K (when over 1,000 exposures remain)

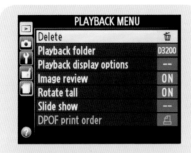

Playback menu
> Delete
> Playback folder
> Playback display options
> Image review
> Rotate tall
> Slide show
> DPOF Print order

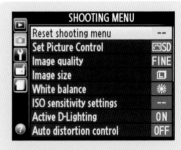

Shooting menu
> Reset shooting menu
> Set Picture Control
> Image quality
> Image size
> White balance
> ISO sensitivity settings
> Active D-Lighting
> Auto distortion control
> Color space
> Noise reduction
> AF-area mode
> Built-in AF-assist illuminator
> Metering
> Movie settings
> Flash cntrl for built-in flash

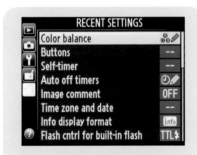

Recent Settings menu

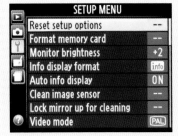

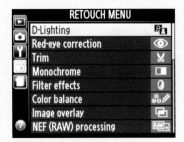

Setup menu
- › Reset setup options
- › Format memory card
- › Monitor brightness
- › Info display format
- › Auto info display
- › Clean image sensor
- › Lock mirror up for cleaning
- › Video mode
- › HDMI
- › Flicker reduction
- › Time zone and date
- › Language
- › Image comment
- › Auto image rotation
- › Image Dust Off ref photo
- › Auto off timers
- › Self-timer
- › Remote on duration
- › Beep
- › Rangefinder
- › File number sequence
- › Buttons
- › Slot empty release lock
- › Print date
- › Storage folder
- › GPS
- › Eye-Fi upload
- › Firmware version

Retouch menu
- › D-Lighting
- › Red-eye correction
- › Trim
- › Monochrome
- › Filter effects
- › Color balance
- › Image overlay
- › NEF (RAW) processing
- › Resize
- › Quick retouch
- › Straighten
- › Distortion control
- › Fisheye
- › Color outline
- › Color sketch
- › Perspective control
- › Miniature effect
- › Selective color
- › Edit movie
- › Side-by-side comparison

Chapter 2
FUNCTIONS

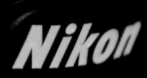

2 FUNCTIONS

For all its promises of simplicity, the Nikon D3200 still sports over a dozen control buttons, a Mode Dial, a Command Dial and a Multi-selector, so it may appear complex and daunting to users familiar with digital compacts or 35mm SLRs. In fact the D3200 is genuinely and thoughtfully designed to be as simple to use as any "point-and-shoot" camera; after all, Nikon has been refining this line of cameras ever since the D40.

When you first unpack it, the D3200 should be set for full auto operation, and at any time you can quickly reset it to this state. To be sure that all settings are restored to their original defaults use the **Reset shooting options** item in the Shooting menu. For a complete reset also use the **Reset** item in the Setup menu *(see pages 96 and 99)*.

However, the D3200 offers much greater flexibility than the average point-and-shoot camera, not to mention far superior image quality. Its intelligent design allows users to make a straightforward, progressive transition

from leaving everything to the camera to taking full control of its many functions. Leaving the camera at default settings misses out on much of its imaging power, and the intention of this chapter is to provide a step-by-step introduction to its most important features and functions. Even in a much longer book it would be impossible to fully explore every last detail, so we'll concentrate on these aspects which will be relevant to the majority of photographers.

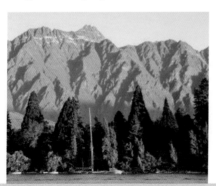

FIRST STEPS ««
When you unpack a new camera, it's tempting to start shooting right away—and, in the end, taking pictures is the best way to learn. However, it still makes sense to peruse this book first, to ensure you don't miss out on new features and functions. *80mm, 1/160 sec., f/8, ISO 400.*

» CAMERA PREPARATION

Some basic operations, like charging the battery and inserting a memory card, are essential before the camera can be used. These operations, and others like changing lenses, may seem trivial, but it's important to be able to perform them quickly and smoothly in awkward situations or when time is short.

Setting the time, date and time zone is also a good idea *(see under Setup menu on page 101).*

› Attaching the strap

To attach the supplied strap, ensure the padded side will face inwards (so the maker's name faces out). Attach either end first to the appropriate eyelet, located at top left and right sides of the camera. Loosen the strap where it runs through the buckle, then pass the end of the strap through the eyelet and back through the buckle. Bring the end of the strap back through the buckle, under the first length of strap already threaded (see photo).

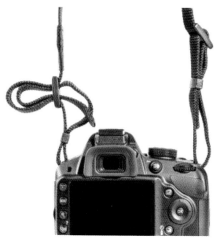

ATTACHING THE STRAP ⌃
On one side the strap is shown threaded but still loose, on the other fully tightened.

Repeat the operation on the other side. Adjust the length as required, but ensure a good length (minimum 2in./5cm) of strap extends beyond the buckle on each side to avoid any risk of it pulling through. When satisfied with the length, pull it firmly to seat it securely within the buckle.

> **Note:**
> This method is not the same as that shown in the Nikon User's Manual, but is both more secure and neater.

2

› Adjusting the diopter

› Mounting lenses

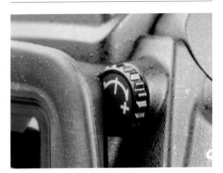

ADJUSTING THE DIOPTER ⌃
Diopter adjustment control.

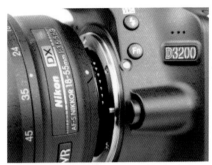

MOUNTING LENSES ⌃
Line up the white dots before inserting.

The D3200 offers dioptric adjustment, between −1.7 and +0.5m^{-1}, to allow for individual variations in eyesight. It's a good idea to optimize this for your eyesight (with glasses or contact lenses if you normally use them) before using the camera. The diopter adjustment control is immediately right of the viewfinder. With the camera switched on, rotate the knob until the viewfinder display (i.e. readouts and focus points) appears sharpest. Unless your eyesight changes, you should only need to do this once. Supplementary viewfinder lenses are available if the built-in adjustment proves insufficient.

Switch the camera OFF before changing lenses. Remove the camera body cap or the lens already mounted. To remove a lens, press the lens-release button and turn the lens clockwise (looking at the front of the camera).To mount a lens, remove the rear lens cap and align the index mark (white dot) on the lens with the one on the camera body, insert the lens gently into the camera and turn it anti-clockwise until it clicks home. Do not use force; if the lens is correctly aligned it will mount smoothly. Most Nikon F-mount lenses can be used safely on the Nikon D3200, however, with older lenses many functions are lost. In particular, autofocus is only available with AF-I and AF-S lenses *(see Chapter 7, page 197)*. With older lenses which have an aperture ring, rotate this to minimum aperture (e.g. f/22) before use.

Warning!

Take care when changing lenses, especially in crowded surroundings or other awkward situations—dropping the lens or the camera is definitely to be avoided! Take extra care in dusty environments and beware wind that could introduce dust or sand while the camera's interior is exposed. Avoid touching the electrical contacts on the lens and camera body, as dirty contacts can cause a malfunction. Replace lens and body caps as soon as possible.

› Inserting and removing a memory card

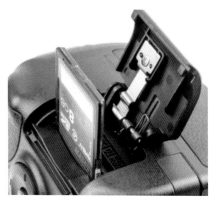

1) Switch OFF the camera and check that the green access lamp on the back of the camera (bottom right) is not lit.

2) Slide the card slot cover on the right side of the camera towards the rear. It will spring open.

3) To remove a memory card, press the card gently into its slot and it will then spring out slightly. Pull the card gently from its slot.

4) Insert a card with its label side towards you and the rows of terminals along the card edge facing into the slot. The "cut-off" corner of the card will be at top left. Push the memory card into the slot, without excessive force, until it clicks home. The green access lamp will light up briefly.

5) Close the card slot cover.

Warning!

Inserting the memory card incorrectly may damage the camera. When the access lamp is lit or blinking do not open the card slot cover or remove the battery.

MEMORY CARD SLOT　　　　　　　　⌃
The D3200 stores images on Secure Digital (SD) cards, including high-capacity SDHC and SDXC type cards.

› Formatting a memory card

It's advisable to format a new memory card, or one that has been used in another camera, before using it with the D3200. Formatting is also the most efficient way to erase existing images on the card, so take care—make sure images have been saved elsewhere before formatting.

To format a memory card

1) Press **MENU** and then select the Setup menu ℉ from the symbols at left of the screen.

2) Select **Format memory card** and press **OK**.

3) Select **Yes** and press **OK**.

› Inserting the battery

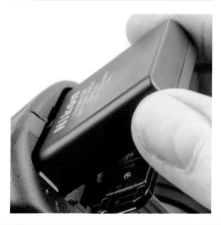

Turn the camera upside down and locate the battery compartment below the hand-grip. Release the latch to open the compartment. Insert the battery, contacts first, with the side that says "Nikon" facing away from the lens. Use the battery to nudge the gold-colored battery latch aside, then slide the battery gently in until the latch locks into position. The green access lamp on the camera back illuminates briefly. Shut the battery compartment cover, ensuring it clicks home.

To remove the battery, switch OFF the camera, and open the compartment cover as above. Press the gold latch to release the battery and pull it gently out of the compartment.

› Battery charging

Use the supplied MH-24 charger to charge the battery. Remove the terminal cover (if present) from the battery and insert the battery into the charger with the maker's name uppermost and terminals facing the contacts on the charger. Press the battery gently but firmly into position. Plug the charger into a mains outlet. The

Charge lamp will blink while the battery is charging, then shine steadily when charging is complete. A completely discharged battery will take around 90 minutes to recharge fully.

› Battery life

Various factors determine how long the battery can last before it needs recharging. Working temperature can be critical and Nikon do not recommend use at temperatures below 0°C or above 40°C. Other factors that can reduce battery life include: heavy use of the LCD screen, e.g. reviewing every image; heavy use of the built-in flash; lots of Live View use; or movie shooting.

Under standard test conditions (CIPA) the D3200 delivers around 550 shots from a fully charged EN-EL14 battery—careful use can more than double this figure, while heavy use can reduce it. The Information Display and viewfinder give an approximate indication of how much charge remains. Battery icons blink when the battery is exhausted.

For information on alternative power sources, see Chapter 8 *(see page 220)*.

Tip

The battery charger can be used abroad (100–240 V AC 50/60 Hz) with a commercially available travel plug adapter. Do not attach a voltage transformer as this may damage the battery charger.

› Switching the camera on

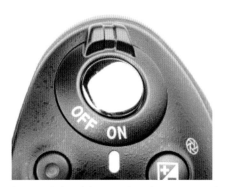

Power switch and shutter-release button

The power switch, which surrounds the shutter-release button, has two settings:

OFF The camera will not operate.
ON The camera operates normally.

2 » BASIC CAMERA FUNCTIONS

With strap, lens, battery, and memory card on board, the camera is ready to shoot. At the outset it will be set to its basic Auto mode *(see page 37)*. The D3200 can shoot indefinitely like this, but as soon as you want to change any settings, review or playback your shots, use Live View or shoot movies, you'll need to use the screen.

In beginning to explore a wider range of options, the key controls are the shutter-release button, Mode Dial, Command Dial and Multi-selector, along with the release mode button.

Settings which are affected by these controls are seen in the Information Display *(see page 32)* on the rear LCD screen, and some are also displayed in the viewfinder. However, in Auto and Scene modes it is perfectly possible (though not necessarily recommended!) to shoot without reference to any of these displays or controls.

› Operating the shutter

The shutter-release button operates in two stages. Pressing it lightly, until initial resistance is felt, activates the metering and focus functions. If you maintain this half-pressure on the button, in Single-servo AF, focus is locked *(see page 54)*. Half-pressure also clears the Information Display, menus or image playback, making

the D3200 instantly ready to shoot. Press the button more firmly (but still smoothly) to take the picture.

› Mode Dial

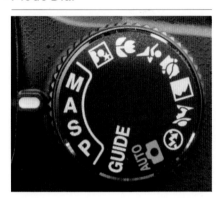

Use this dial to choose a mode, deciding whether the camera operates automatically or requires input. There are 13 possible positions, which fall into four groups: Full Auto modes, User-control modes, Scene modes and Guide mode. See under Exposure modes *(page 36)* and Guide mode *(page 76)*. To operate, simply rotate to the chosen position.

Warning!

The Mode Dial does not have a lock and accidental shifts into a different mode can occur.

› Command Dial

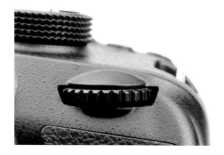

The Command Dial falls naturally under the right thumb when the camera is in the shooting position. It is fundamental to the operation of the Nikon D3200, especially in the user-control modes.

Operating the Command Dial

The dial's function is flexible, varying according to the operating mode at the time. In Shutter-priority (S) or Manual (M) mode, rotating the Command Dial selects the shutter speed. In Aperture-priority (A) mode it selects the aperture. In program (P) mode it engages flexible program, changing the combination of shutter speed and aperture. For descriptions of these modes *see page 43*.

When shooting in Full Auto modes or Scene modes, the Command Dial on its own has no effect.

› Multi-selector

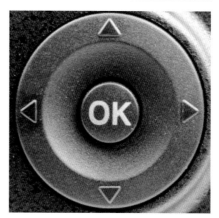

The other principal control is the Multi-selector. Its main use when shooting pictures is to select and change settings in the Information Display, moving up, left, right, or down. The **OK** button at its center is used to confirm settings. The Multi-selector is also used for navigating through the menus, and through images on playback—these will be covered in the relevant sections.

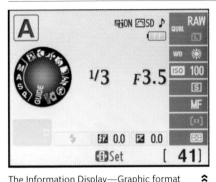

The Information Display—Graphic format ⌃

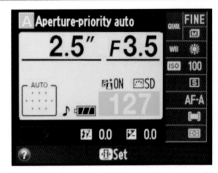

The Information Display—Classic format ⌃

The Information Display is central to using the Nikon D3200. If you're familiar with traditional camera control using buttons and dials it may seem a little strange at first, but soon proves to be a straightforward, though arguably slower, way of accessing camera functions.
To activate the Information Display, use any of these methods:

— Half-press and release the shutter-release button (if you maintain pressure the Information Display will not appear).

— Press the **INFO** button on top of the camera.

— Press the **⚏▸** button on the rear of the camera.

This brings up a display showing the selected exposure mode, the aperture and shutter speed, and a range of other detail. This screen can be displayed in a choice of two formats. **Graphic** format, which is active by default, uses icons and pictures to illustrate the effect of various settings. Alternatively, **Classic** format presents the information in a more traditional, mostly numerical, way. The color scheme can also be changed. These options are chosen through the Setup menu (see page 99).

Screen orientation
When using the Information Display, the camera detects whether it is being held in landscape or portrait orientation and sets the display accordingly.

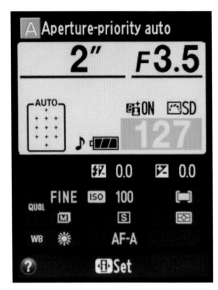

The Information Display in portrait orientation ⌃

› Active Information Display

The ⟨i⟩ button ⌃

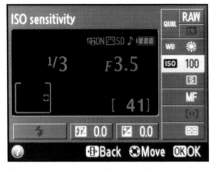

The Active Information Display with ⌃
ISO setting highlighted

The initial Information Display is passive—it displays key camera settings but does not allow you to change them. To make changes possible, press ⟨i⟩ while the initial display is visible (if the screen is blank, press the button twice). The screen changes and the Multi-selector can now be used to move quickly through the various settings. To make changes, press **OK**, and the range of options for that setting appears. Use the Multi-selector to move through these options. When the one you want is highlighted, press **OK** again to select it.

> **Note:**
> The term "Active Information Display" is used for this screen throughout this book. It is not used in Nikon's own manual. You can't use the **INFO** button on top of the camera to access the Active Information Display.

› Release mode

The release mode button ⌃

"Release mode" may seem a slightly obscure term. It determines whether the camera takes a single picture or shoots continuously, and can also allow the shot to be delayed.

Selecting Release mode

1) Press ⊟ to bring up the menu of options (see table opposite). (This screen can also be reached from the Active Information Display: Release mode is halfway down the right-hand side.)

2) Highlight the desired option and press **OK** to make it active. The chosen release mode is shown in the Information Display.

Six possible release modes can be selected in this way.

› Buffer

Images are initially stored in the camera's internal memory ("buffer") before being written to the memory card. The maximum number of images that can be recorded in a continuous burst depends upon file quality, release mode, memory card capacity, and how much buffer space is available. The figure for the number of burst frames possible at current settings is shown in the viewfinder at bottom right when the shutter-release button is half-depressed. e.g. **[r05]**.

If **(0)** appears, the buffer is full, and no more shots will be taken until enough data has been transferred to the memory card to free up space in the buffer. This normally happens very quickly but you may need to release pressure on the shutter-release button momentarily before shooting will resume.

> **Note:**
> When the shutter-release button is not depressed, the figure at bottom right shows the total number of images for which space remains on the memory card at current size/quality settings. In some cases this may be more than 1000, in which case the figure is followed by a K—for example, [1.9]K = 1900 images possible.

RELEASE MODE OPTIONS

Setting	Description
S **Single frame**	The camera takes a single shot each time the shutter release is fully depressed.
Continuous	The camera fires continuously as long as the shutter release is fully depressed. The maximum frame rate is 4fps.
Self-timer	The shutter is released a set interval after the release button is depressed. Can be used to minimize camera shake and for self-portraits. The default interval is 10 sec. but 2, 5 or 20 sec. can be set using Custom Setting c3.
2s **Delayed remote**	Requires the optional ML-L3 remote control; shutter fires approx 2 sec. after remote is tripped.
Quick response remote	Requires the optional ML-L3 remote control; shutter fires immediately when remote is tripped.
Q **Quiet shutter release**	Similar to Single frame, but mirror remains up and shutter does not re-cock until shutter-release button is released, making operation almost silent.

2 » EXPOSURE MODES

The choice of exposure mode makes a significant difference to the amount of control you can—or can't—exercize. Exposure modes are selected from the Mode Dial, on top of the camera. The D3200 has a wide choice of exposure modes but they can be conveniently divided into three main groups: Full Auto modes, Scene modes and User-control modes.

Guide mode

Guide mode is also selected from the Mode Dial but is not in itself an exposure mode; instead it helps you make a guided selection from the available exposure modes. For more on Guide mode *see page 76*.

In Full Auto modes and Scene modes the majority of settings are controlled by the camera. These go beyond basic shooting settings (shutter speed and aperture) to include options such as release mode, whether or not flash can be used, and how the camera processes the shot. The difference is that Full Auto modes use compromise settings to cover most eventualities while Scene mode settings are tailored to particular shooting situations.

User-control modes, by contrast, give you complete freedom to control virtually everything on the camera.

Mode group	Exposure mode		
Full Auto modes	AUTO	Auto	Leave all decisions about settings to the camera.
	🚫	Auto (flash off)	
Scene modes	👤	Portrait	Choose the appropriate mode to suit the subject, and the camera then employs appropriate settings.
	🏔	Landscape	
	👶	Child	
	🏃	Sports	
	🌷	Close-up	
	🌃	Night portrait	
User-control modes	**P**	Program	Allow much greater control over the full range of camera settings.
	S	Shutter-priority	
	A	Aperture-priority	
	M	Manual	

» FULL AUTO MODES

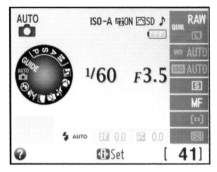

In its manual, Nikon calls these "Point and Shoot" modes, which is probably a fair reflection of the way they're likely to be used. It works pretty well, most of the time; you'll hardly ever get a shot that doesn't "come out" at all, but you may find that the results aren't always exactly what you were aiming for. After all, it's the camera, not you, that's deciding what kind of picture you are taking and how it should look.

There's only one difference between these two modes. In ░ Auto mode the built-in flash will pop up automatically if the camera determines light levels are too low, and can only be turned off via the Active Information Display *(see page 33).* (If a separate accessory flashgun is attached and switched on, this overrides the built-in unit.)

In ░ Auto (flash off) mode the flash stays off no matter what. This is useful whenever flash is banned or would be intrusive, or when you just want to discover what the D3200 can do in low light.

CANDID CAMERA ░

Full auto mode is ideal when shots need to be grabbed quickly, but can diminish your sense of creativity and satisfaction. *55mm, 1/800 sec., f/7.1, ISO 400.*

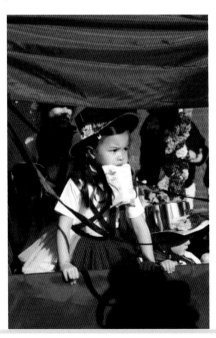

2

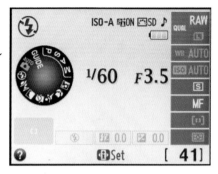

› Exposure warnings

In all modes, if the camera detects that light levels are too low—or, more rarely, too high—for an acceptable exposure, a warning will be displayed in both the viewfinder and the Information Display. The viewfinder display blinks, and **Lo** or **Hi** appears in place of the shutter speed indication. In the Information Display you'll see both a flashing question mark and a warning message such as "Subject is too dark." Pressing ⊶ brings up a more detailed message.

The camera will still take pictures, but results may be underexposed or subject to camera shake (if it's too dark) or overexposed (if too light).

If conditions are too dark, two useful options are to fit a different lens with a wider maximum aperture, or to increase the ISO sensitivity *(see page 67)*.

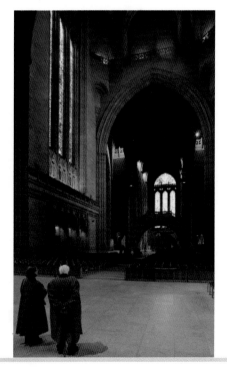

SHOT IN THE DARK **«**
Auto (flash off) mode is suitable when flash is banned or would be disruptive. *14mm, 1/20 sec., f/6.3, ISO 1600, braced against pillar.*

» SCENE MODES

The Nikon manual calls these Creative Photography modes: a debatable tag, as they take many decisions out of your hands. However, even the most experienced may find them handy on occasion, as a quick way to set the camera for shooting a particular kind of image. Newcomers to DSLR photography will find Scene modes an ideal way to discover how differently the camera can interpret the same scene. This makes them a great stepping stone to the full range of options offered by the D3200. The first step is to understand how the various Scene modes work and to be aware of the difference they can make in your images: an obvious way to do this is to shoot the same subject using different modes.

Scene modes control basic shooting parameters such as focusing, shutter speed and aperture. They also determine how the image is processed by the camera (assuming you are shooting JPEG images, *see page 61*). For instance, Nikon Picture Controls *(see page 87)* are predetermined. In 🀫 Portrait mode, for example, the camera applies a Portrait Picture Control, which gives natural color rendition and is kind to skin tones.

PORTRAIT »
Portrait mode is naturally suitable for "people" pictures, but turning off the flash is usually a good idea. *46mm, 1/40 sec., f/3.2, ISO 400.*

› 🀫 Portrait

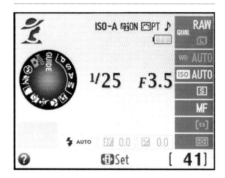

In Portrait mode the camera sets a relatively wide aperture to reduce depth of field, helping subjects stand out from their background. The camera also selects the

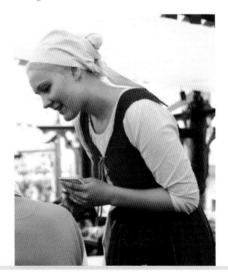

focus point automatically (presumably using Face Detection technology), though you can switch to manual selection. The flash automatically pops up if the camera determines light levels are too low, but can (and often should) be turned off via the Active Information Display. Attaching a separate flashgun will override the built-in flash—and usually improves results dramatically *(see page 160)*.

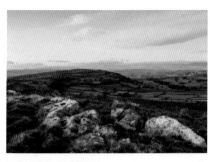

STRENGTH IN DEPTH ⏫
Landscape mode keeps foreground and back-ground sharp. *20mm, 1/13 sec., f/11, ISO 100.*

› ⛰ Landscape

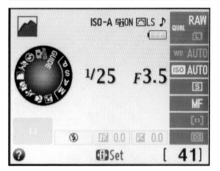

In Landscape mode, the camera sets a small aperture, maximizing depth of field *(see page 119)*. This means that shutter speeds can be slow, so a tripod is advisable. The camera selects the focus point automatically, but this can be overridden. A Landscape Picture Control is applied for vibrant colors. The built-in flash is off, even in low light (you can't activate it manually) but you can use a separate flashgun.

› 👶 Child

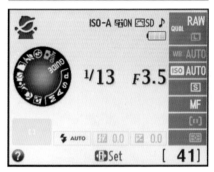

Child mode is broadly similar to Portrait mode, but one obvious difference is that the camera tends to set higher shutter speeds as children are less likely than adults to sit still when required. Colors are also handled slightly differently to produce results that are more vivid overall but still give natural skin tones. You can, of course, use it for adult portraits too,

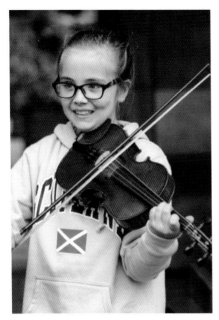

QUICK KIDS ⌃
Child mode is slanted towards active subjects rather than static poses. *150mm, 1/800 sec., f/2.8, ISO: 200.*

if you prefer a more vibrant result or the subject is active. The flash activates automatically, but can be turned off via the Active Information Display.

NEED FOR SPEED »
Sports mode aims to freeze the action. *150mm, 1/500 sec., f/8, ISO: 200.*

› 🏃 Sports

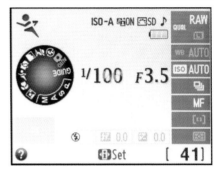

Sports mode is intended for shooting not just sports but other fast-moving subjects, including wildlife. The camera will set a fast shutter speed to freeze the action. This usually implies a wide aperture and therefore shallow depth of field. The camera initially selects the central focus point and if it detects subject movement will track it using the other 10 focus points. (You can also override this initial selection yourself.) The flash remains off, even in low light, and there's no way to override this, except by attaching a separate flashgun.

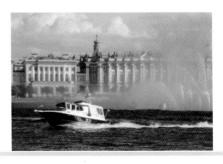

❋ Close-up

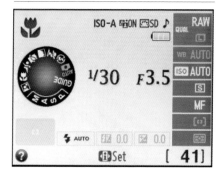

Close-up mode is of course intended for shooting at really close range. The camera sets a medium to small aperture to improve depth of field, so a tripod is often useful to avoid camera shake. The built-in flash will activate automatically in low light, but fortunately it can be turned off via the Active Information Display; built-in flash is often a poor choice for close-up shots (*see*

FLOWER SHOT
Close-up mode is versatile but it's often best to turn flash off. *55mm, 1/320 sec., f/6.3, ISO 400.*

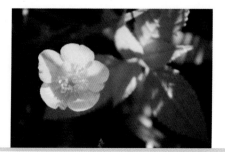

page 174). A separate accessory flashgun, attached and switched on, will override the built-in unit. The camera automatically selects the central focus point, but this can be overridden, using the Multi-selector *(see page 58)*. For much more on close-up photography, see Chapter 5 *(see page 166)*.

⬛ Night portrait

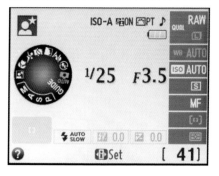

Night portrait mode is similar to regular Portrait mode, but when the ambient light is low it allows the camera to set a long shutter speed (up to 30 sec.) to allow an image of the background to register. It's therefore best to use a tripod. The built-in flash operates automatically, but can be turned off, or a flashgun attached.

This mode would be a reasonable choice for night-time landscapes as well as portraits, but it's then even more likely that you'll want to turn the flash off. The image is processed using a Portrait Picture

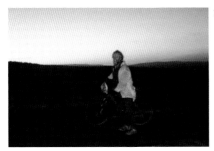

NIGHT CYCLE ⌃
The flash illuminates the figure while the overall exposure is long enough for the fading sunset to register. *32mm, 1/20 sec., f/8, ISO 3200.*

Control, to favor skin tones rather than to give vivid results from city skylines. The camera will set a wide aperture—for greater depth of field or a long exposure, use Manual (M) mode.

Taking the picture

Basic picture taking is essentially the same in all Full Auto and Scene modes.

1) Select the desired mode by rotating the Mode Dial to the appropriate position.

2) Frame the picture.

3) Half-depress the shutter-release button to activate focusing and exposure. The focus point(s) will be displayed in the viewfinder image, and shutter speed and aperture settings will appear at the bottom of the viewfinder.

4) Fully depress the shutter-release button to take the picture.

» USER CONTROL MODES

The remaining four modes are traditional standards, which will be familiar to any experienced photographer. As well as allowing direct control over the basic settings of aperture and shutter speed (even in P mode through flexible program), these modes give full access to controls like White Balance *(see page 63)*, Active D-Lighting *(see page 86)* and to Nikon Picture Controls *(see page 87)*. These extra controls give you lots of influence over the look and feel of the image.

› (P) Programmed auto

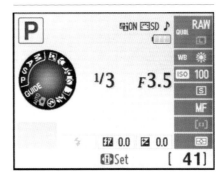

In P mode the camera sets a combination of shutter speed and aperture that will give correctly exposed results in most situations. The same is true in Full Auto and Scene modes, but P mode allows you to adjust other parameters to suit your own creative ideas, including white balance *(see page*

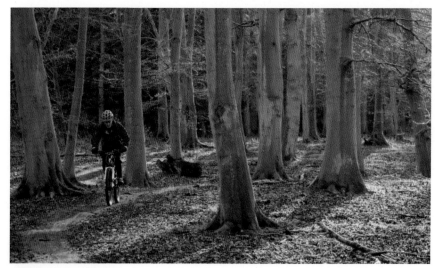

THROUGH THE WOODS
Programmed auto mode gives you much more scope to tailor camera settings to suit your own creative ideas. *70mm, 1/320 sec., f/5, ISO 800.*

63) and Nikon Picture Controls *(see page 87)*. You can change things even more in P mode through options like flexible program *(see below)*, exposure lock *(see page 51)* and exposure compensation *(see page 50)*, and you have complete freedom to use flash, or not, as you wish.

1) To use (P) Programmed auto mode, rotate the Mode Dial to position P.

2) Frame the picture.

3) Half-depress the shutter-release button to activate focusing and exposure. The focus point(s) will be displayed in the viewfinder image and shutter speed and aperture settings will appear below the viewfinder image.

4) Fully depress the shutter-release button to take the picture.

Flexible program

Without leaving P mode you can change the combination of shutter speed and aperture by rotating the Command Dial. While flexible program is in effect the **P** indication in the Information Display changes to **P***. The shutter speed/aperture combination in the viewfinder can be seen to change.

› (S) Shutter-priority auto

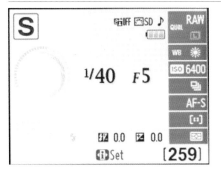

Tip

Sports mode, in particular, aims to set a fast shutter speed. This is fine up to a point, but does not give the direct and exact control that S mode does. S mode also allows quick shifts to a much slower shutter speed, which can be a great way to get a more impressionistic view of action. See page 123 for more about shutter speeds.

In Shutter-priority (S) mode, you control the shutter speed while the camera sets an appropriate aperture to give correctly exposed results in most situations. Control of shutter speed is key for moving subjects *(see page 123)*. Shutter speeds between 30 seconds and 1/4000 second can be set. Fine-tuning of exposure is possible through exposure lock *(see page 51)*, exposure compensation *(see page 50)*, and possibly auto bracketing *(see page 52)*.

1) To use (S) Shutter-priority auto, rotate the Mode Dial to position S.

2) Frame the picture.

3) Half-depress the shutter-release button to activate focusing and exposure. The focus point(s) will be displayed in the

viewfinder image and shutter speed and aperture settings will appear below the viewfinder image.

4) Rotate the Command Dial to alter the shutter speed; the aperture will adjust automatically.

5) Fully depress the shutter-release button to take the picture.

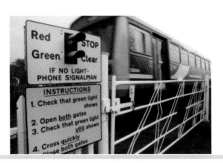

SPEED CONTROL   »
Shutter-priority auto allows direct control of shutter speed. *18mm, 1/160 sec. f/11, ISO 200.*

› (A) Aperture-priority auto

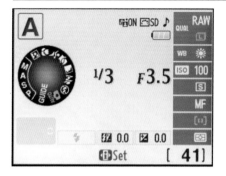

1) To use (A) Aperture-priority auto mode, rotate the Mode Dial to position A.

2) Frame the picture.

3) Half-depress the shutter-release button to activate focusing and exposure. The focus point(s) will be displayed in the viewfinder, and shutter speed and aperture settings will appear below the viewfinder image.

4) Rotate the Command Dial to alter the aperture; the shutter speed will adjust automatically. The Information Display (in Graphic mode) also shows a graphic representation of the aperture.

5) Fully depress the shutter-release button to take the picture.

In Aperture-priority (A) mode, you control the aperture while the camera sets an appropriate shutter speed to give correctly exposed results in most situations. Control of aperture is particularly useful for regulating depth of field *(see page 119)*. The range of apertures available is limited by the lens that's fitted, not by the camera. Fine-tuning of exposure is possible through exposure lock *(see page 51)*, exposure compensation *(see page 50)*, and possibly bracketing *(see page 52)*.

SEED SHOW »
Aperture-priority mode is ideal for controlling depth of field. *50mm macro, 1/1200 sec., f/8, ISO 200.*

› (M) Manual mode

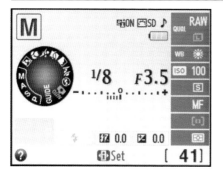

In M mode, you control both shutter speed and aperture for maximum creative flexibility. Manual mode is most comfortably employed when shooting without pressure of time or in fairly constant light conditions. Many experienced photographers use it habitually to retain complete control.

Shutter speeds can be set to any value between 30 seconds and 1/4000 second. There's also B (or "bulb"), in which the shutter remains open indefinitely as long as you keep the shutter-release button depressed.

The range of apertures available is determined by the lens in use.

1) To use (M) Manual mode, rotate the Mode Dial to position M.

2) Frame the picture.

3) Half-depress the shutter-release button to activate focusing and exposure. The focus point(s) will be displayed in the viewfinder image and shutter speed and aperture settings will appear at the bottom of the viewfinder. Check the analog exposure display in the center of the viewfinder readouts and if necessary adjust shutter speed and aperture, or both, to achieve correct exposure.

4) Rotate the Command Dial to alter the shutter speed.

5) Hold 🗲 and rotate the Command Dial to alter the aperture.

6) Fully depress the shutter-release button to take the picture.

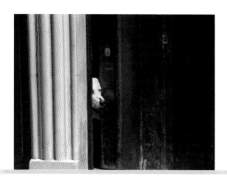

DOG IN THE DOOR ««
I used Manual mode and checked the histogram and highlights displays. Fortunately the dog remained where it was for the few seconds I needed. *70mm, 1/160 sec., f/8, ISO 200.*

2 › Using Analog exposure displays

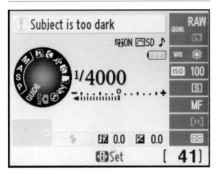

Analog exposure display in the Information Display, showing significant underexposure (note the exposure warning to the same effect)

In Manual mode, an analog exposure display appears in the viewfinder readouts, and in the Information Display if it's active. This shows whether the photograph would be under- or overexposed at the current settings. Adjust shutter speed and/or aperture until the indicator is aligned with the **0** mark in the center of the display.

Tip

In any User control mode, not just Manual, it is always helpful—time permitting—to review the image and check the histogram display (see Playback page 93) after taking the shot (a process now known as "chimping"). If necessary you can then make further adjustments for creative effect or if the camera's recommended exposure does not achieve the desired result.

» METERING MODES

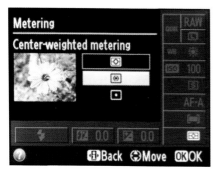

Metering mode selection in the Active Information Display

The measurement of light levels (metering) to ensure that images are correctly exposed is a vital function. The D3200 provides three different metering modes, which should cover any eventuality. Switch between them using the Metering item in the Active Information Display. This is only possible in P, S, A or M modes—in all other modes matrix metering is automatically selected.

› ☒ 3D color matrix metering II

Using a 420-segment color sensor, 3D Color Matrix Metering II analyzes data on the brightness, color and contrast of the scene. When used with Type G or D Nikkor lenses, the system also analyzes distance information based on where the camera focuses—that's why it's called 3D. With other CPU lenses, this distance information

is not used and metering automatically reverts to Color Matrix Metering II.

Matrix metering is recommended for the vast majority of shooting situations and will generally produce excellent results.

› ☒ Center-weighted metering

This very traditional form of metering will be familiar to most experienced photographers. The camera measures light from the entire image area, but gives greater importance to a central circle. Center-weighted metering is useful in portraiture, where the key subject often occupies the central portion of the frame. However, the D3200 still employs matrix metering when in Portrait mode.

› ☒ Spot metering

In this mode the camera meters solely from a small circular area centered on the current focus point, allowing you to meter from an off-center subject. This does not apply if Auto-area AF (AF-A) is in use, when the metering point is the center of the frame. Spot metering can be useful where an important subject is much darker or lighter than the background and you want to be sure it is correctly exposed (matrix metering is more likely to compromise between subject and background).

2 » EXPOSURE COMPENSATION

The D3200 will produce accurate exposures under most conditions, but no camera is infallible. It certainly can't read your mind or anticipate your creative ideas.

All metering systems still work partly on the assumption that key subject areas have a middling tonal value (like the "gray card" inside the cover of this book), and should appear as a mid-tone in the images. With subjects a long way from mid-tone, this can give inaccurate results. We've all seen brilliant white snow turn out gray: normal metering has tried to reproduce it as mid-tones, making it darker than it should be. Where very dark tones predominate, the converse is true.

Tip

Exposure compensation is only available in P, S, and A modes. In M mode 🔲 *controls the aperture; in the remaining modes exposure control is fully automatic.*

The Nikon manual suggests that exposure compensation is most appropriate when using center-weighted or spot metering. However, even matrix metering is not infallible, and there's no reason not to use exposure compensation here too.

In the days of film, considerable experience was needed to accurately anticipate the need for exposure compensation. With their instant feedback on exposure, digital cameras smooth the learning curve. It's always helpful—time permitting—to check the image, and specifically the histogram, after shooting *(see page 93)*. This makes it much easier to see when exposure compensation is needed. With experience, you can recognize in advance when the need may arise.

The basic principle for exposure compensation is very simple: to make the subject look lighter, give more exposure—in other words, apply positive compensation. And conversely, to make the subject darker (to keep dark tones looking dark), give less exposure—in other words, apply negative compensation.

› Resetting exposure compensation

Remember to reset exposure compensation (Step 4 below) when you no longer need it. Exposure compensation is canceled when you switch to Full Auto or Scene modes, but the camera remembers the compensation setting and restores it when you revert to the User control modes. It does not reset automatically

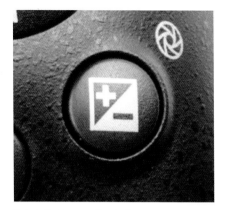

Exposure compensation button

even when the camera is switched off. However, like many other settings, exposure compensation will be restored to zero by a reset *(see page 69)*.

› Using exposure compensation

1) Press ⊞ and rotate the Command Dial to set the negative or positive compensation required (between –5 Ev and +5 Ev). Alternatively, the Active Information Display can be used.

2) Release ⊞. The chosen exposure compensation value is shown in the Information Display. In the viewfinder, the **0** at the center of the Analog Exposure Display flashes while compensation is in effect.

3) Take the picture as normal. If time allows, check that the result is satisfactory.

4) To restore normal exposure settings, repeat step 1 until the displayed value returns to **0.0**.

› Exposure lock

Exposure lock is another way to fine-tune the camera's exposure setting—in fact, many users find this the quickest and most intuitive method. It's useful, for instance, in situations where very dark or light areas (especially light sources) within the frame can over-influence exposure. Exposure lock allows you to meter from a more average area, by pointing the camera in a different direction or stepping closer to the subject, then hold that exposure while re-framing the shot you want. Unlike exposure compensation, it can be used in Scene modes.

> **Note:**
> Nikon does not recommend using exposure lock when you're using matrix metering, but don't let that stop you if matrix metering does not produce the desired result.

› Using exposure lock

1) Aim the camera in a different direction, or zoom the lens to avoid the potentially problematic dark or light areas. If you're using center-weighted or spot metering, look for areas of middling tone (but which are receiving the same sort of light as the main subject).

2) Half-press the shutter-release button to take a meter reading, then keep it pressed as you press **AE-L/AF-L** to lock the exposure value.

3) Keep **AE-L/AF-L** pressed as you reframe the image and shoot in the normal way.

By default, **AE-L/AF-L** locks focus as well as exposure. This can be changed using the **Buttons** item in the Setup menu. There are several options, but the most relevant for using exposure lock is **AE Lock only**. You can also opt for **AE Lock (hold).** In this case you can release **AE-L/AF-L** after step 2, and exposure will remain locked until you press **AE-L/AF-L** again, or the meters turn off. (For more on the **Buttons** item *see page 103*).

› Exposure bracketing

A time-honored way to ensure that an image is correctly exposed is to take several frames at differing exposures, and select the best one later—this is known as exposure bracketing. Unlike other Nikon DSLRs, the D3200 does not have an automatic bracketing facility, so bracketing must be done manually.

In P, S, and A exposure modes, the easiest way to employ manual exposure bracketing is using exposure compensation *(see page 50)*. For example, take one shot at the recommended exposure, another with exposure compensation at −1 Ev and a third at +1 Ev. It is definitely quicker to use the ⊠ button and Command Dial for this, rather than the Active Information Display.

> **Tip**
>
> *Apart from acting as an insurance policy (to ensure you have the exposure right for any given shot), experimenting with exposure bracketing is a great way to get a feel for what exposure really means. Use a tripod to make sure all shots are framed alike.*

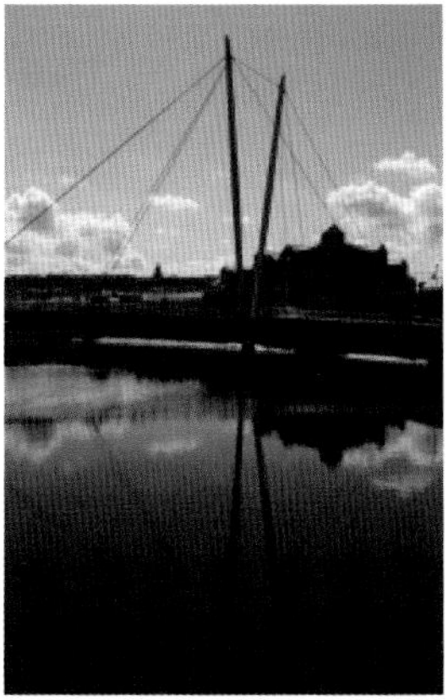

-1 Ev

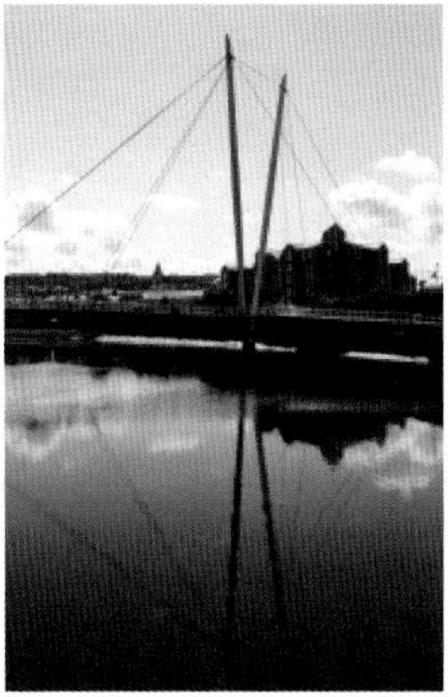

0 Ev

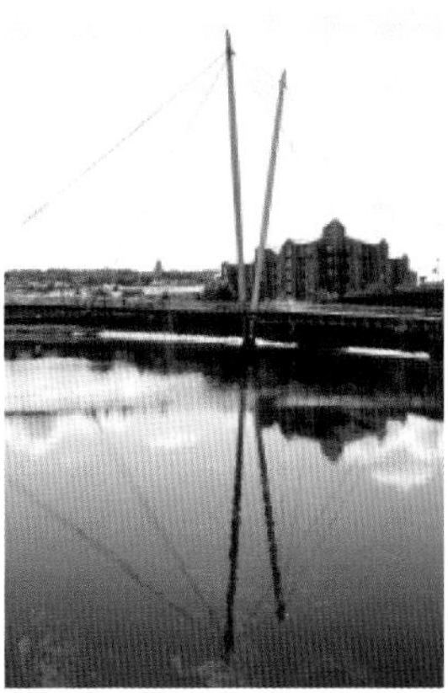

1 Ev

ON REFLECTION »

Exposure bracketing: –1 Ev; 0 Ev; +1 Ev. *24mm, varying shutter speed, f/11, ISO 200, tripod.*

With a little practice it takes only a second or two to rattle off three (or more) shots.

In M exposure mode you bracket by directly changing either the aperture or shutter speed. For instance, if the recommended exposure is 1/60 sec. at f/11, changing the shutter speed to 1/125 sec. is equivalent to –1 Ev and 1/30 sec. is equivalent to +1 Ev.

There's no real way to bracket exposure in Scene modes.

Tip

Bracketing is not limited to three shots—that's just an example. You can take as many shots as you like. Exposure compensation allows any range up to +/– 5 Ev, but in Manual mode you can range even further.

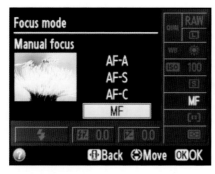

Focus mode selection

Focusing is not simply about ensuring that "the picture" is in focus. It's actually quite difficult, sometimes impossible, to ensure that everything in an image appears sharp. The first essential is making sure that the camera focuses on the desired subject, or sometimes—especially in close-up photography—the right part of the subject. Control of depth of field *(see page 119)* helps to determine how much of the rest of the image will also be sharp.

To secure focus on the desired subject, the D3200 has flexible and powerful focusing capabilities, offering manual focus as well as a range of autofocus modes.

› To select the focus mode

1) In the Active Information Display, select the focus mode item (by default this reads **AF-A**) about halfway down the right-hand side.

2) Press **OK** and then select from the available options; press **OK** again to confirm the selection and return to shooting mode.

If the camera is in an Auto or Scene mode, the Active Information Display only shows two options. Manual focus can always be selected, but the only autofocus option is **AF-A**. In P, S, A or M mode, four options are available.

› AF-A (Auto-servo AF)

By default the camera is set to AF-A in all exposure modes. AF-A means that the camera automatically switches between the two autofocus modes, single-servo AF and continuous-servo AF.

› AF-S (Single-servo AF)

The camera focuses when the shutter-release button is pressed halfway. Focus remains locked on this point as long as the shutter release remains depressed. The shutter cannot release to take a picture unless focus has been acquired (focus priority). This mode is recommended for accurate focusing on static subjects.

› AF-C (Continuous-servo AF)

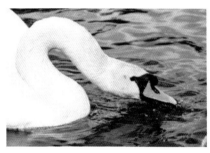

SWAN TAKE ✱
AF-C is recommended for moving subjects.
105mm, 1/400 sec., f/11, ISO 200.

In this mode, the camera continues to seek focus as long as the shutter release is depressed: if the subject moves, the camera will refocus. The camera is able to take a picture even if perfect focus has not been acquired.

The D3200 employs predictive focus tracking—if the subject moves while AF-C is active, the camera analyzes the movement and attempts to predict where the subject will be when the shutter is released.

› (M) Manual focus

When a camera has sophisticated AF capabilities, manual focus might appear redundant, but many photographers still value the extra control and involvement. There are also certain subjects and circumstances which can bamboozle even the best AF systems. Manual focusing is a straightforward process, which hardly requires description: set the focus mode to MF and use the focusing ring on the lens to bring the subject into focus.

> **Tip**
>
> *Many lenses have an A/M switch— setting this to M will automatically set the camera's mode to MF.*

› The electronic rangefinder

When using a lens that does not focus automatically with the D3200, you can still take advantage of the camera's focusing technology thanks to focus confirmation. It requires an appropriate focus area to be selected, as if you were using autofocus. When the subject in that area is in focus a green dot appears at far left of the viewfinder data display.

You can obtain further assistance with manual focus by choosing **ON** for the

Rangefinder item in the Setup menu. This enables the exposure display in the viewfinder to show whether the focus point is in front of or behind the subject, and by how much. (This is not available in Manual exposure mode, when the exposure indicator is needed for its primary purpose.)

› AF-area modes

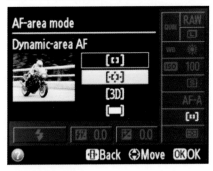

AF-area mode selection

The D3200 has 11 focus points, which are indicated by small black rectangles in the viewfinder. When you half-press the shutter release, the currently active focus point(s) are highlighted in red.

When using autofocus, the AF-area mode determines which of these focus points the camera will employ—in other words, what the camera will focus on.

Auto-area (see below) is the default setting in most shooting modes, but can always be changed. However, the camera

only "remembers" this change in P, S, A or M modes. If you change AF-area mode in any of the Auto or Scene modes it will remain in effect only as long as you remain in that exposure mode. For instance, if you switch from Portrait to Landscape and then back again, you'll find that the camera has reverted to Auto-area.

Many photographers prefer to make their own selection; determining what the subject is seems a pretty basic decision. AF-area mode options can be selected in the Shooting menu, but it's usually easier to use the Active Information Display.

› Auto-area AF [■]

In Auto-area AF, the camera selects the focus point automatically. In effect, the camera decides what the intended subject is. When type G or D lenses are used, Face Recognition allows the D3200 to distinguish human subject(s) from the background.

› Single-point AF [⊡]

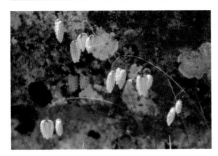

TOP SEED ⌃
I took care to focus on the closest of the seed-heads and let the background go a little soft.
70mm, 1/250 sec., f/8, ISO 160.

In this mode, you select the focus area, using the Multi-selector to move quickly through the 11 focus points. The chosen focus point is outlined in the viewfinder. This mode is best suited to relatively static subjects.

› Dynamic-area AF [⊡]

Dynamic-area AF is available when using AF-C mode (continuous-servo AF). The initial focus point is still selected by the user, as in single-area AF, but if the subject moves, the camera will then employ other focus points to maintain focus (provided you keep the shutter release semi-depressed). This mode is naturally best suited to moving subjects, but particularly if they remain generally in line with the initial focus point.

› 3D tracking (11 points) [3D]

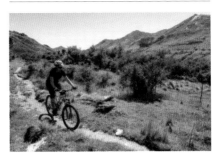

CYCLE TRACK ⌃
3D tracking is best for subjects moving both towards the camera and across the field of view.
14mm, 1/640 sec., f/9, ISO 400.

This mode, too, is available when using AF-C continuous-servo AF. Again, the initial focus point is still selected by the user. However, if the subject moves, 3D tracking uses a wide range of information, including subject colors, to maintain focus as long as you keep the shutter release semi-depressed. This mode is probably your best bet for subjects moving across the field of view.

» FOCUS POINTS

The D3200 has 11 focus points covering most of the central area of the image frame, which means you can generally make a quick and precise selection to focus accurately on any subject.

› Focus point selection

1) Ensure the camera is set to an AF-area mode other than Auto-area.

2) Half-depress the shutter-release button to activate the autofocus system.

3) Using the Multi-selector, move the focus point to the desired position (pressing **OK** jumps directly to the central focus point). The chosen focus point is briefly highlighted in red.

4) Press the shutter-release button halfway to focus at the desired point; depress it fully to take the shot.

› Focus lock

Though the D3200's focus points cover a wide area, they do not extend to the edges of the frame, and sometimes you may need to focus on a subject that does not naturally coincide with any of the focus points. To do this, the simplest procedure is as follows:

1) Adjust framing so that the subject falls within the available focus area.

2) Select an appropriate focus point and focus on the subject in the normal way.

3) Lock focus. In Single-servo AF mode, this can be done either by keeping half-pressure on the shutter-release button, or by pressing and holding **AE-L/AF-L**. An **AE-L** icon appears in the viewfinder. In Continuous-Servo AF, only **AE-L/AF-L** can be used to lock focus.

BEAK FOCUSING   ⌄
Shifting the focus point gives very different results. *200mm, 1/1600 sec., f/5.6, ISO 200.*

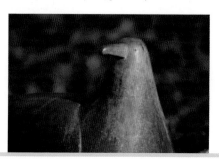
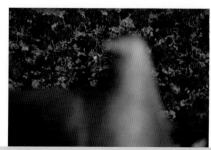

4) Reframe the image as desired and press the shutter-release button fully to take the picture. If you maintain half-pressure on the shutter-release button (in Single-servo AF), or keep **AE-L/AF-L** under pressure (in either AF mode), focus will remain locked for further shots.

Note:

By default, **AE-L/AF-L** also locks exposure as well as focus, but this behavior can be changed using the **Buttons** item in the Setup menu *(see page 103).*

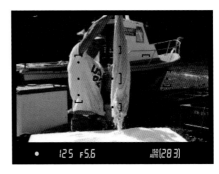

The viewfinder displays available focus areas and an in-focus indicator at the left of the menu bar

ON THE BEACH ☇
The D3200's focusing system makes it easy to select your subject and lock focus manually.

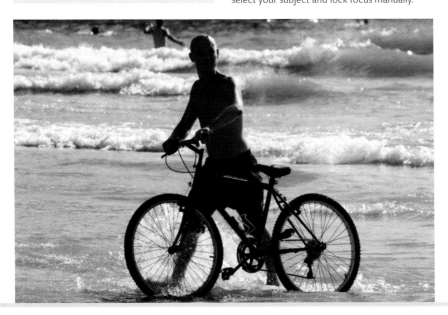

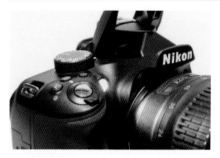

AF-assist illuminator

An AF-assist illuminator—a long name for a small lamp—is available to help the camera focus in dim light. It requires the camera to be in Single-Servo AF (AF-S). It will then illuminate automatically when required, except in Landscape and Sports modes, where it is disabled. The AF-assist illuminator can be turned **OFF** for all modes through the **Built-in AF-assist illuminator** item in the Shooting menu. It is also off in Live View and Movie shooting.

For effective operation, the lens should be in the range 18–200mm and the subject distance should be between 1ft 8in.–9ft 10in. (0.5–3m).

» IMAGE QUALITY

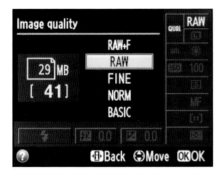

The Image quality settings are not a shortcut to great pictures—that is still, thank goodness, the photographer's responsibility. "Image quality" refers to the file format, i.e. the way in which image data is recorded. The D3200 offers a choice of two file types: NEF (RAW) and JPEG.

The essential difference is that JPEG images are extensively processed in the camera to produce photos that should be usable right away (for instance, for direct printing from the memory card), needing little or no further processing on computer.

NEF (RAW) files, on the other hand, record the raw data from the camera's sensor "as is", without processing in the camera; this leaves much greater scope for processing on the computer to achieve the desired pictorial result. This requires sophisticated software such as Nikon Capture NX2 or Adobe Photoshop. Because they preserve the raw data, the generic term for this kind of file is RAW or Camera RAW. NEF is a specific file format used by Nikon for RAW files.

The D3200 allows two versions of the same image to be recorded simultaneously, one RAW and one JPEG. The JPEG can be used as a quick reference file for immediate needs while the RAW version can be processed later for the ultimate result.

There are three options for JPEG quality (the compression applied when the file is saved). More compression produces smaller files but can degrade image quality. Fine produces the largest files but highest quality; Basic produces smaller files but lower quality; Normal is in between.

Setting image quality

1) In the Active Information Display, select the **QUAL** item at top right of the screen.

2) Press **OK** to bring up the list of options. Using the Multi-selector, highlight the required setting then press **OK** again to make it effective.

Image quality options

RAW	12-bit NEF (RAW) files are recorded for the ultimate quality and flexibility.
FINE	8-bit JPEG files are recorded with a compression ratio of approximately 1:4; should be suitable for prints of A3 size or even larger.
NORM	8-bit JPEG files are recorded with a compression ratio of approximately 1:8; should be suitable for modest-sized prints.
BASIC	8-bit JPEG files are recorded with a compression ratio of approximately 1:16, suitable for transmission by email or website use but not recommended for printing.
RAW + F	Two copies of the same image are recorded simultaneously, one NEF (RAW) and one JPEG Fine.

» IMAGE SIZE

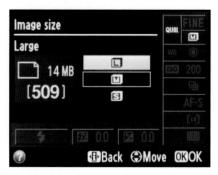

Setting image size in the Active Information Display

There are three options for JPEG image size. **Large** is the maximum available size, i.e. 6016 x 4000 pixels. **Medium** is 4512 x 3000 pixels, equivalent to a 12-megapixel camera. **Small** is 3008 x 2000 pixels,

equivalent to a 6-megapixel camera. Small images exceed the maximum resolution of an HD TV or most computer monitors, and yield good prints up to A4 size (at 200 dpi).

Setting image size

1) In the Active Information Display, select **Image size**, immediately below **Image quality** at top right of the screen. Alternatively, select **Image size** in the Shooting menu. (If Image quality is set to **RAW** or **RAW+FINE**, you will not be able to select this item by either method.)

2) Press **OK** to bring up the list of options. Using the Multi-selector, highlight the required setting then press **OK** again to make it effective.

» WHITE BALANCE

Light sources, natural and artificial, vary enormously in color. The human eye and brain are very good (though not perfect) at compensating for this and seeing people and objects in their "true" colors, so that we nearly always see grass as green, and so on. Digital cameras also have a capacity to compensate for the varying colors of light and, used correctly, the D3200 can produce natural-looking colors under almost any conditions you're ever likely to encounter.

The D3200 has a sophisticated system for determining white balance (WB) automatically, which produces very good results most of the time. For finer control, or for creative effect, the D3200 also offers a range of user-controlled settings, but these are only accessible when using P, S, A, or M modes.

> **Note:**
> When shooting RAW images, the in-camera white balance setting is not crucial, as white balance can also be adjusted in post-processing using suitable software. However, it's still helpful to get it right as it affects how images look on playback and review.

› Setting white balance

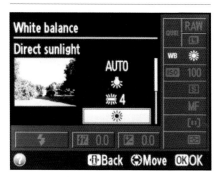

Setting white balance in the Active Information Display

There are two ways to set white balance:

Using the Active Information Display

1) In the Active Information Display, select the **WB** item near top right and press **OK** to reveal a list of options.

2) Use the Multi-selector to highlight the required setting, then press **OK** to accept it.

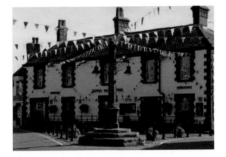

Incandescent

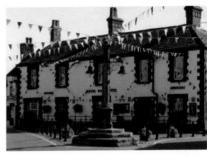

Flash

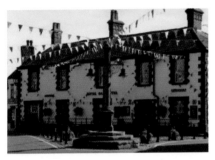

Cool-white fluorescent

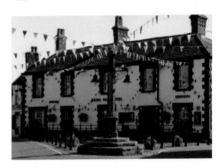

Cloudy

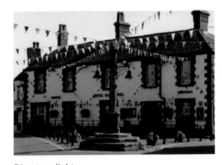

Direct sunlight

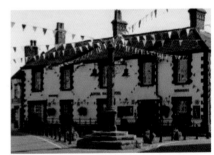

Shade

EFFECTS OF WHITE BALANCE SETTINGS

Six otherwise identical shots, taken seconds apart, demonstrate how radically White Balance settings can change the overall effect.

Using the Shooting menu

This is a slower method but makes extra options available.

1) Press **MENU**, select **Shooting menu** and navigate to **White Balance**.

2) Press **OK** to reveal a list of options.

3) Use the Multi-selector to highlight the required setting, then press **OK**.

4) In most cases, a graphical display appears. This lets you fine-tune the setting using the Multi-selector—or just press **OK** to accept the standard value. When you select **Fluorescent**, however, a sub-menu appears, from which you can select an appropriate variety of fluorescent lamp *(see the table on the next page)*.

Notes:
If you use the the Active Information Display to select **Fluorescent**, the precise value will be whatever was last selected in the sub-menu under the Shooting menu. (The default is 4: **Cool-white fluorescent**.)

Energy-saving bulbs, which have largely replaced traditional incandescent (tungsten) bulbs, are compact fluorescent units. Their color temperature varies but many are rated around 2700°K, equivalent to Fluorescent setting 1: **Sodium-vapor lamps**. In case of doubt, it's always a good idea to take test shots if possible, or allow for adjustment later by shooting RAW files.

Tip

If images consistently appear color-shifted on your computer screen, don't try and compensate by adjusting the camera's white balance; the problem is far more likely to be with the computer screen settings (see page 234).

2

Icon	Menu option	Color temperature	Description
AUTO	Auto	3500–8000	Camera sets white balance automatically, based on information from imaging and metering sensors. Most accurate with Type G and D lenses.
☀	Incandescent	3000	Use in incandescent (tungsten) lighting, e.g., traditional household bulbs.
	Fluorescent:	Submenu offers seven options:	
	1 Sodium-vapor lamps	2700	Use in sodium-vapor lighting, often employed in sports venues.
	2 Warm-white fluorescent	3000	Use in warm-white fluorescent lighting
	3 White fluorescent	3700	Use in white fluorescent lighting
☀	4 Cool-white fluorescent	4200	Use in cool-white fluorescent lighting
	5 Day white fluorescent	5000	Use in daylight white fluorescent lighting
	6 Daylight fluorescent	6500	Use in daylight fluorescent lighting
	7 High temp. mercury-vapor	7200	Use in high color temperature lighting, e.g., mercury vapor lamps.
☀	Direct sunlight	5200	Use for subjects in direct sunlight
⚡	Flash	5400	Use with built-in flash or separate flashgun. Value may require fine-tuning with large-scale studio flash.
☁	Cloudy	6000	Use in daylight, under cloudy/overcast skies.
⌂	Shade	8000	Use on sunny days for subjects in shade
PRE	Preset Manual	n/a	Derive white balance direct from subject or light source, or from an existing photo.

ISO SENSITIVITY SETTINGS

The ISO setting governs the camera's sensitivity to greater or lesser amounts of light. At higher ISO settings, less light is needed to capture an acceptable image. As well as accommodating lower light levels, higher ISO settings are also useful when you need a small aperture for increased depth of field *(see page 119)* or a fast shutter speed to freeze rapid movement *(see page 123)*. Conversely, lower ISO settings are useful in brighter conditions, and/or when you want to use wide apertures or slow shutter speeds. The D3200 offers ISO settings from 100 to 3200. Image noise *(see page 141)* does tend to increase at higher settings, but the D3200 controls it well.

There is an additional setting, **Hi 1**, equivalent to 12,800 ISO. This is recommended with reservations, as image noise does become more noticeable. By default, the D3200 sets the ISO automatically. You can also set it manually, except in Full Auto modes. This new setting will continue to apply if you switch exposure modes. However, if you switch to P, S, A, or M mode and then back to a Scene mode, the camera reverts to Auto-ISO. The camera only permanently "remembers" manual settings in P, S, A, or M modes.

GET YOUR GOAT
Shooting handheld in shady woodland on a dull day, a high ISO setting was essential to catch this wild goat. *105mm, 1/100 sec., f/5.6, ISO 1600.*

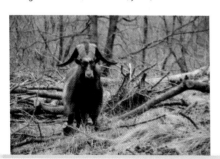

› Setting the ISO

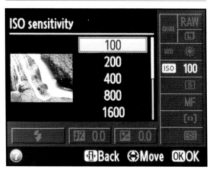

Setting the ISO in the Active Information Display

The usual way to set the ISO is through the Active Information Display:

1) In the Active Information Display, select the **ISO** item on the right and press **OK** to reveal a list of options.

2) Use the Multi-selector to highlight the required setting, then press **OK** to accept it.

Alternatively, use the **ISO sensitivity settings** item in the Shooting menu.

A third option is available, by assigning the **Fn** button to **ISO sensitivity** through the **Buttons** item in the Setup menu. If this is done, pressing the button brings up the ISO item in the Information Display and you can then change settings very quickly by rotating the Command Dial. If you change ISO settings regularly, this is an option well worth considering.

› Auto ISO sensitivity

The **ISO sensitivity settings** item in the Shooting menu has a sub-menu called Auto ISO sensitivity control. If this is set to **ON**, the D3200 will automatically depart from a manually selected ISO if it determines that this is required for correct exposure. Extra options within this menu allow you to limit the maximum ISO and minimum shutter speed which the camera can employ when applying Auto ISO sensitivity control.

» COLOR SPACE

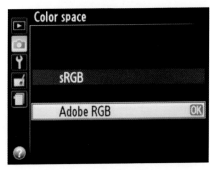

Setting Color space in the Shooting menu

Color spaces define the range (or gamut) of colors which can be recorded. Like most DSLRs, the Nikon D3200 offers a choice between sRGB and Adobe RGB color spaces. The chosen color space will apply to all shots taken in all exposure modes.

sRGB (the default setting) has a narrower gamut but images often appear brighter and more punchy. It's the standard color space for online use and in photo printing stores, and is a safe choice for images likely to be used or printed straight off, with little or no post-processing.

Adobe RGB has a wider gamut and is commonly used in professional printing and reproduction. It's a better choice for images that are destined for professional applications, especially in print, or where significant post-processing is anticipated.

To select the color space, use the **Color space** item in the Shooting menu.

» QUICK RESET

The D3200 offers a quick way to reset a large number of camera settings (listed below) to default values. The top item in the Shooting menu is **Reset shooting menu**, and similarly the top item in the Setup menu is **Reset setup options**. In each case, select **Yes** and then press **OK** to reset all affected options to their default values. The settings covered by these reset items are listed below.

For more detail on Shooting menu items not already covered, *see pages 96–98*; for more detail on Setup menu items not already covered, *see pages 99–106*.

Item	Default setting		
Reset shooting menu			
Set Picture Control	Standard settings only		
Image quality	JPEG Normal		
Image size	Large		
White balance	Auto (fine-tuning off)		
ISO sensitivity	Auto and scene modes	Auto	
	User-control modes	100	
	Auto ISO sensitivity	100	
Active D-Lighting	On		
Auto distortion control	Off		
Color space	sRGB		
Noise reduction	On		
AF-Area mode	♣		Single-point AF
—Viewfinder	⚡		Dynamic-area AF
	⚡, ⊕, ♨, 🏔, 📷, ⚡, P, S, A, M		Auto-area AF
AF-Area mode	⚡, ⊕, ♨, 🏔, 📷, ⚡,		Face-priority AF
—Live View and Movie	⚡, P, S, A, M		Wide-area AF
	♣		Normal-area AF
AF-assist	On		
Metering	Matrix		
Movie Settings	Quality	1920 x 1080; 24fps	
	Sound	On	

Item	Default setting	
Built-in flash	TTL	
Focus point	Center	
Flexible program	Off	
AE-L/AF-L button hold	Off	
Focus mode	Viewfinder	AF-A
	Live View/movie	AF-S
Flash mode	📷ᴬᵁᵀᴼ , 🌼 , 🌷 , 🕯	Auto
	🌃	Auto slow sync
	P, S, A, M	Front-curtain sync
Exposure compensation	Off	
Flash compensation	Off	
Reset setup options		
Resets almost all Setup menu options including the following (directly related to shooting):		
LCD brightness	0	
Info display format	Graphic; background color green	
Self-timer delay	10 secs	
Beep	On	
Rangefinder	Off	
Buttons	Fn	ISO sensitivity
	AE-L/AF-L	AE/AF lock
	AE lock	Off
Date imprint	Off	
Eye-Fi upload	Enable	

» LIVE VIEW

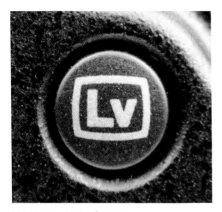

Live View activation button

Live View mode enables users to frame pictures using the LCD screen rather than the viewfinder, in the same way as most compact digital camera users. However, Live View on DSLRs has generally been seen as secondary to the viewfinder. DSLRs are essentially designed around the viewfinder and it still has many advantages for the majority of picture-taking—it's more intuitive and offers the sense of a direct connection to the subject, carries much less risk of camera shake, and viewfinder-based autofocus is faster. It can also be very hard to see the screen in bright sunlight, unless you use a shade *(see Chapter 8 Accessories and care, page 214).*

However, Live View has definite advantages in some circumstances.

The screen image shows 100% of the picture area, which the viewfinder does not; this is clearly better for precise framing. Also, Live View focusing, though noticeably slower than viewfinder AF, is more accurate. These advantages are fully realized when the camera is on a tripod— which also neutralizes much of the viewfinder's advantage in handling.

Live View is also the jumping-off point for shooting movies with the D5000. Movies are covered in Chapter 6 *(see page 176)*; however, familiarity with Live View is a big help in preparing you for movie shooting.

› Using Live View

To activate Live View, press the **Lv** button on the rear of the camera. The mirror flips up, the viewfinder blacks out, and the rear monitor screen displays a continuous live preview of the scene. A range of shooting information is displayed at top and bottom of the screen, partly overlaying the image. Pressing **INFO** changes this Information Display, cycling through a series of screens as shown in the table: a further press returns to the starting screen.

Live View info	Details
Show indicators (default)	Information bars superimposed at top and bottom of screen.
Show movie indicators	Information for movie shooting superimposed; movie frame area also indicated.
Hide indicators	Top information bar disappears, key shooting information still shown at bottom.
Framing grid	Grid lines appear, useful for critical framing.

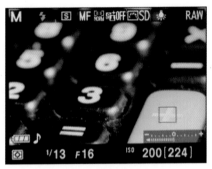

Live View display options include detailed settings info (Show indicators)

Press the shutter-release button fully to take a picture, as when shooting normally. If you're shooting in Continuous release mode, the mirror stays up, and the monitor remains blank between shots, making it hard to follow moving subjects.

If Auto or Scene modes are selected, exposure control is fully automatic, except exposure level can be locked by pressing and holding **AE-L/AF-L**. In P, S, A, or M modes, exposure levels can be adjusted by

±5 Ev using ![icon], and the Live View display changes to reflect this. Shutter speed and aperture settings can also be changed in the usual way, and again the Live View display changes accordingly. The D3200 is one of the first Nikon DSLRs where Live View gives a realistic preview of the final image. To exit Live View press **Lv** again.

> ## Focusing in Live View

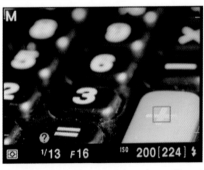

The focus area (red rectangle) can be positioned anywhere on screen

Focusing in Live View operates differently from normal shooting—because the mirror is locked up, the usual focusing sensor is unavailable. Instead, the camera reads focus information directly from the main image sensor. This is slower than normal AF operation (often very noticeably so), but very accurate. You can also zoom in the view, which helps in placing the focus point exactly where you want it (and in manual focusing too).

Live View has its own set of autofocus options, with two AF modes and four AF-area modes.

> ### Live View AF modes

The AF-mode options are Single-servo AF (AF-S) and and Full-time servo AF (AF-F). AF-S corresponds to AF-S in normal shooting: the camera focuses when the shutter release is pressed halfway, and focus remains locked as long as the shutter-release button remains depressed.

AF-F corresponds roughly to AF-C in normal shooting. However, the camera continues to seek focus as long as Live View remains active. When you press the shutter-release button halfway, focus will lock, and remains locked until you release the button or take a shot.

Select Live View AF mode as follows:

1) Activate Live View by pressing **Lv**.

2) Press ◄**B**► to engage the Active

Information Display. Select the focus item (about halfway down the right-hand side).

3) Select AF-S or AF-F and press **OK**.

4) Press ◄**B**► again to return to Live View.

> ### Live View AF-area mode

AF-area modes determine how the focus point is selected. Live View AF-area modes do not correspond to the ones used in normal shooting. See the table for details of the four Live View AF-area modes. Again, selection is through the Active Information Display.

Select the Live View AF-area mode as follows:

1) Activate Live View with **Lv**.

2) Press ◄**B**► to engage the Active Information Display and select the AF-area mode (half-way down the right-hand side).

3) Select the desired option and press **OK**.

4) Press ◄**B**► again to return to Live View. Alternatively, Live View AF-area mode can be selected in the Shooting menu.

AF Mode	Description
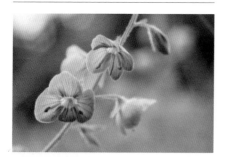 Face priority	Uses face detection technology to identify portrait subjects. Double yellow border appears outlining such subjects. If multiple subjects are detected the camera focuses on the closest. Default in 🅰, 🌼, 🏃, 🌷, 🏞, 🌃 .
WIDE Wide-area	Camera analyzes focus information from area approx ⅛ the width and height of the frame; area is shown by red rectangle. Default in P, A, S, M, 🏃 .
NORM Normal area	Camera analyzes focus information from a much smaller area, shown by red rectangle. Useful for precise focusing on small subjects. Default in 🌷 .
Subject tracking	Camera follows selected subject as it moves within the frame.

› Using Live View AF

to zoom closer. Helpfully, the zoom centers on the focus point. Once the focus point is set, autofocus is activated as normal by half-pressing the shutter-release button. The red rectangle turns green when focus is achieved.

🅾️ Face-priority AF

When this mode is active, the camera automatically detects up to 35 faces and

FOCUS ACCURACY ⌃
Normal area AF is the best choice for precision and accuracy.

WIDE Wide-area AF and NORM Normal area AF

In both these AF-area modes, the focus point (outlined in red) can be moved anywhere on the screen, using the Multi-selector in the usual way. Pressing ⊕ zooms the screen view—press repeatedly

Tip

The ability to move the focus point anywhere on screen is useful for off-center subjects, especially when using a tripod. In normal handheld shooting it's quicker and easier to use the viewfinder and employ focus lock (see page 58).

selects the closest. The selected face is outlined with a double yellow border. You can override this and focus on a different person by using the multi-selector to shift the focus point. To focus on the selected face, press the shutter-release button halfway.

⊕ Subject tracking

When you select Subject tracking, a white rectangle appears at the center of the screen. Align this with the desired subject (by moving the camera or using the Multi-selector) then press **OK**. The camera "memorizes" the subject and the focus target then turns yellow. It will now track the subject as it moves, and can even reacquire the subject if it temporarily leaves the frame. To focus, press the shutter-release button halfway. The target rectangle blinks green as the camera focuses and then becomes solid green. If the camera fails to focus the rectangle blinks red instead. Pictures can still be taken but focus may not be correct. To end focus tracking press **OK** again.

› Manual focus

Manual focus is engaged as in normal shooting *(see page 55)*. However the Live View display continues to reflect the previously selected Live View AF mode. It's helpful to have Wide-area AF or Normal-area AF selected, as the display still shows a rectangle of the appropriate size. If you zoom in for more precise focusing, the zoom centers on the area defined by the rectangle; this can be a great help in close-up work and other occasions when you need really precise focusing.

Warning!

Subject tracking isn't fast enough for rapidly moving subjects. Using the viewfinder is much more effective for these.

2 » GUIDE MODE

Guide mode is selected from the Mode Dial like the various Exposure modes but, as already observed, it is not in itself an Exposure mode. Instead, Guide mode is intended to guide less experienced users through some of the available options, not only for shooting but also for playback and for camera set-up. That word "some" is significant—Guide mode caters for various common scenarios but falls well short of covering all the possibilities that the camera can tackle.

› Guide menu

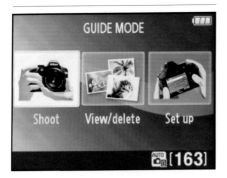

The Guide menu—opening screen

To enter Guide mode, rotate the Mode Dial to **GUIDE**. The Guide menu screen appears. To return to this screen if the monitor turns off, or from the Information Display, press **MENU** (this only works while the Mode Dial is in the **GUIDE** position).

The opening screen offers three choices: **Shoot**, **View/Delete**, and **Setup**—initially, **Shoot** is highlighted. Use ▶ and ◀ to select the desired option and press **OK** to enter.

› Guide menu—Shoot

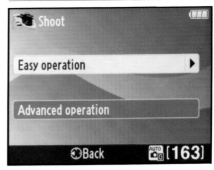

The Guide menu—Shoot options

The Shoot screen offers two options: **Easy operation** and **Advanced operation**. Move between them with ▲ and ▼; use ▶ or **OK** to enter.

Easy operation

Enter this and the camera offers another series of choices (see the table opposite). Each leads to one of the Auto or Scene modes, though the Guide menu uses different terminology for some of them. Once you're familiar with the Scene modes, it will be obvious that selecting

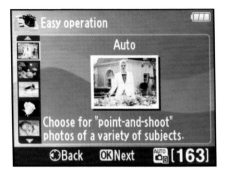

The Guide menu—Easy operation

them directly via the Mode Dial is a much quicker method; making a choice through the Guide menu takes multiple button presses, and usually the Multi-selector too.

Having selected a mode, press **OK**. This brings up an explanatory screen.

Lightly press the shutter-release button to start shooting, or press **OK** to bring up another screen showing some further options. These are **Start shooting**, **Use live view**, **Shoot movies**, and **More settings**. The first three are largely self-explanatory, though **Shoot movies** takes you into Live View and you must press O to start recording video.

Select **More settings** and press **OK** to see some more choices. These will include **Release mode** and **ISO sensitivity**, and in most cases also **Flash mode**. As you scroll through the available options the Guide menu provides a brief explanation and an image of an appropriate subject. Having made your choices, lightly press the release button to start shooting.

Guide menu—Easy operation

Guide menu heading	Exposure mode	Notes	Flash mode selection
Auto	🔺 Auto		Available
No flash	🚫 Auto (flash off)		Unavailable
Distant subjects	🏃 Sports	Uses Sports mode to maintain high shutter speed, preventing camera shake with long lenses.	Unavailable
Close-ups	🌷 Close up		Available
Sleeping faces	👶 Child	Unlike regular Child mode (i.e. set from Mode dial) flash is Off by default, but can be changed in **More settings**.	Available
Moving subjects	🏃 Sports		Unavailable
Landscapes	🏔 Landscape		Unavailable
Portraits	👤 Portrait		Available
Night portrait	🌃 Night portrait		Available

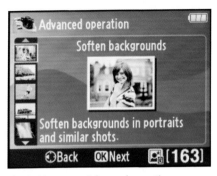

The Guide menu—Advanced operation

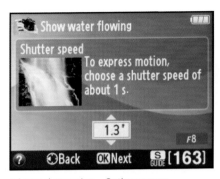

Advanced operation—Options screen

Advanced operation

Select **Advanced operation**, and the next screen shows a list of choices—you need to scroll down to see them all (see the table opposite). Make a choice by pressing ▶ and you'll see a screen explaining which Exposure mode comes into force. You can now lightly press the shutter-release button to start shooting, or press ▶ again to move to another screen where you can change a key camera setting for each scenario (shutter speed, aperture, white balance, exposure compensation or ISO sensitivity). Once you start shooting, further alterations to these settings are made in the normal way—e.g. using the Command Dial to change the aperture.

Tip

The Freeze motion screens suggest shutter speeds of 1/200 sec. for people and 1/1000 sec. for vehicles. This is all very well, but 1/200th sec. isn't going to give you a sharp image of a speeding cyclist, while 1/1000 sec. could be more than fast enough for many vehicles (e.g. a bus in normal traffic conditions!) The implicit assumption that vehicles need a faster shutter speed than people is naive to say the least—but you have to start somewhere.

Guide menu—Advanced operation

Guide menu heading	Exposure mode	Notes	See page for more info
Soften backgrounds	A	Final screen allows you to set aperture using ▲ and ▼;advises a wide aperture such as f/4.	*See pages 46, 119*
Bring more into focus	A	Final screen allows you to set aperture using ▲ and ▼; advises a wide aperture such as f/16; advises fitting a lens of 24mm or wider.	*See pages 46, 119*
Freeze motion (people)	S	Final screen allows you to set shutter speed using ▲ and ▼; advises 1/200 sec. or faster.	*See pages 45, 123*
Freeze motion (vehicles)	S	Final screen allows you to set shutter speed using ▲ and ▼; advises 1/1000 sec. or faster.	*See pages 45, 123*
Show water flowing	S	Final screen allows you to set shutter speed using ▲ and ▼; advises about 1 sec.	*See pages 45, 124*
Capture reds in sunsets	P	Selects "direct sunlight" for white balance; final screen allows fine-tuning of white balance setting.	*See pages 43, 63*
Take bright photos	P	Sets exposure compensation to +1; final screen allows you to change level of compensation.	*See pages 43, 50*
Take dark (low key) photos	P	Sets exposure compensation to –1; final screen allows you to change level of compensation.	*See pages 43, 50*
Reduce blur	P	Engages Auto ISO sensitivity control; final screen allows you to set minimum shutter speed and upper limit for Auto ISO range.	*See pages 43, 67*

Further options

Having made any changes, once more you can lightly press the shutter-release button to start shooting. Alternatively, press **OK** to bring up another screen (as in Easy Operation) showing the **Start shooting**, **Use live view**, **Shoot movies**, and **More settings** options.

More settings includes the following: **Flash compensation**; **Release mode**; **ISO sensitivity settings**; **Set Picture Control** *(see page 87)*; **Exposure compensation** *(see page 50)* and **White Balance** *(see page 63)*. Select any of these and press ▶ to bring up relevant options, though the choices may be limited (e.g. **Set Picture Control** only offers Standard, Vivid and Monochrome). From this options screen, press ◀ to go back to the main **More settings** screen (in some cases you'll need to use **OK** instead). At any point, pressing the shutter-release button takes you into shooting mode.

› Guide menu—View/delete

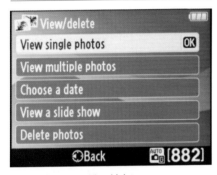

The Guide menu—View/delete

This section of the Guide menu offers an alternative way to access some of the D3200's playback functions. These are all described in the following pages under **Image playback** and **Playback menu**; there's no need to repeat the information here. The Guide menu headings are:

—**View single photos** (see page 82);
—**View multiple photos** (see Viewing images as thumbnails, page 84: the Guide menu initially shows four images at a time);

—**Choose a date** (see Calendar View, page 85)
—**View a slide show** (see Slide show, page 94)
—**Delete photos** (see Deleting images, page 91).

› Guide menu—Setup

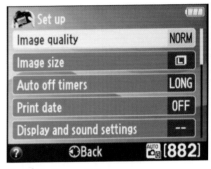

The Guide Menu—Setup

This section of the Guide menu gives access to a range of settings that would otherwise be accessed through the Playback menu (see page 91), Shooting menu (see page 96), and Setup menu (see page 99); a couple are also accessible through the Active Information Display (see page 32).

Guide menu—Advanced operation

Guide menu heading		Normal menu location	Accessible through Active Information Display
Image quality		Shooting menu *(see page 96)*	Yes
Image size		Shooting menu *(see page 96)*	Yes
Auto off timers		Setup menu *(see page 103)*	No
Print date		Setup menu *(see page 104)*	No
Display and sound settings	Monitor brightness	Setup menu *(see page 99)*	No
	Info background color	Setup menu *(see page 99)*	No
	Auto info display	Setup menu *(see page 99)*	No
	Beep	Setup menu *(see page 103)*	No
Movie settings		Shooting menu *(see page 98)*	No
Output settings	HDMI	Setup menu *(see page 100)*	No
	Video mode	Setup menu *(see page 100)*	No
Playback folder		Playback menu *(see page 92)*	No
Playback display options		Playback menu *(see page 93)*	No
DPOF print order		Playback menu *(see page 95)*	No
Clock and language		Setup menu *(see page 101)*	No
Format memory card		Setup menu *(see page 99)*	No
Slot empty release lock		Setup menu *(see page 104)*	No

Note:
When you set the Mode Dial to **GUIDE**, pressing **MENU** brings up the Guide menu and access to the normal camera menus is unavailable.

2 » IMAGE PLAYBACK

The D3200's large, bright LCD screen makes image playback a pleasure, and it's also full of helpful information. At default settings, the most recent image is automatically displayed immediately after shooting, as well as whenever ▶ is pressed. If **Image review** is set to **Off** in the Playback menu, images are not automatically displayed. If you're using Continuous release mode, playback only begins after the last image in a burst has been captured; images are then shown in sequence.

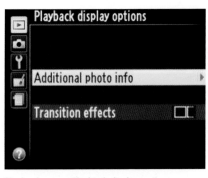

Playback menu: Playback display options

> ## Viewing additional pictures

To view images on the memory card, other than the one most recently taken, scroll through them using the Multi-selector. Scroll right to view images in the order of capture, scroll left to view in reverse order ("go back in time"). You can choose to have images slide or fade into each other when you do this by visiting **Transition effects** under **Playback display options** in the Playback menu.

> ## Viewing photo information

The D3200 records masses of information (metadata) about each image taken, and this can also be viewed on playback, using the Multi-selector to scroll (up or down) through up to six pages of information. To make the following pages available, go to the Playback menu: select **Playback display options**, then select **Additional photo info**. To make available three detailed pages of Shooting data, ensure that **Data** is checked. To make the Highlights display available (see below), select check **Highlights**. To make the RGB histogram display available (see next page), check **RGB histogram**. To see an overview page which includes basic information and a simplified histogram, check **Overview**. To apply these changes, scroll up to **Done** and press **OK**.

If all options are unchecked, playback will only show a full-screen view with minimal data below.

› Highlights

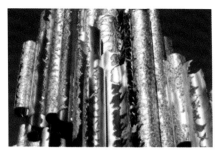

HIGHLIGHT FANTASTIC ⌄
I wanted to ensure that this image had plenty of sparkle, but didn't want to lose too much detail in clipped highlights, so checked the highlight display after the first shot. *56mm, 1/200 sec., f/14, ISO 100.*

› Histogram displays

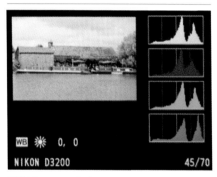

RGB histogram display

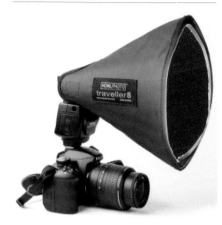

The Highlights display (this image is taken from Adobe Lightroom, and the highlights are shown in red; in the display on the camera back these areas would flash black).

The Highlights screen displays a flashing warning for any areas of the image with "burnt-out" highlights, i.e. areas that are completely white with no detail recorded *(see page 131).* This gives a useful check on whether an image is correctly exposed, and it's more objective than relying solely on a general impression of the image on the monitor.

The histogram is a kind of graph showing the distribution of dark and light tones in an image. As a way of assessing if an image is correctly exposed it's much more precise than just looking at the full-frame playback, especially in bright sunlight, when it's hard to see the screen image clearly. The overview page *(see page 82)* shows a single histogram during playback. By selecting **Playback mode** in the Playback menu and checking **RGB histogram**, you gain access to a more detailed display which shows individual histograms for the three color channels (red, green, and blue). The histogram display is the single most useful feature of image playback and it's normally the first thing I look at. Learning to interpret the histogram is a massive help in getting the best results from your D3200. For more on this, *see Chapter 3 In the Field, page 116.*

> ## Playback zoom

To assess sharpness, or for other critical viewing, it's possible to zoom in on a section of an image. For Large images (including RAW files) the maximum magnification is approximately 27x.

1) Press ⊕ to zoom in on the image currently displayed (or the selected image in Thumbnail View). Press repeatedly—up to nine times—to increase the magnification; press ⊖ to reduce it. A small navigation window appears briefly, with a yellow outline indicating the area currently visible in the monitor.

2) Use the Multi-selector to move the zoom area, i.e. to view other areas of the image.

Tip

The highest magnification levels (eight and nine presses on ⊕) appear pixelated. For assessing sharpness, there's little to be gained by going beyond seven presses.

3) Rotate the Command Dial to view equivalent areas of other images at the same magnification.

4) To return to full-frame viewing, press the **OK** button to return instantly to full-frame view. Or exit playback by pressing ▶ or the shutter-release button.

> ## Viewing images as thumbnails

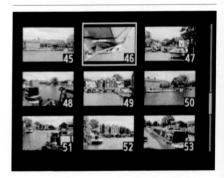

Thumbnail View

To view more than one image at a time, press ⊖ once to display four images, twice for nine images, three times for

72 images. Use the Multi-selector to scroll up and down to bring other images into view. The currently selected image is outlined in yellow. To return to full-frame view, press **OK**.

› Calendar View

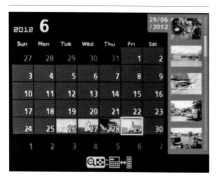

Calendar View

An extension to thumbnail view, Calendar View can display images grouped by the date(s) when they were taken. Having pressed Q🔳 repeatedly to display 72 images, press once more to reach the first calendar page (date view). The most recent date is highlighted, and pictures from that date appear in a vertical strip on the right (the thumbnail list). In this view, the Multi-selector can be used to navigate to different dates.

If you press Q🔳 again, you highlight the thumbnail list for the selected date and can then scroll through pictures taken on that day. Press Q to see a larger preview of

the currently selected image. Press Q🔳 again to go back to date view. Press **OK** at any point to return to full-frame view.

› Deleting images

To delete the current image, or the selected image in Thumbnail View, press 🗑. A confirmation dialog appears. To proceed with deletion press 🗑 again. To cancel, press ▶.

In Calendar View (date view) you can also delete all images taken on a selected date. Highlight that date in Date View, then press 🗑; when the confirmation dialog appears press 🗑 again to delete or ▶ to cancel.

› Protecting images

To protect the current image, or the selected image in Thumbnail View/ Calendar View, against accidental deletion, press **AE-L/AF-L**. To remove protection, press **AE-L/AF-L** again.

Warning!

Protected images will be deleted when the memory card is formatted.

» IMAGE ENHANCEMENT

The D3200 enables you to adjust and enhance images in various ways right there in-camera. These adjustment options divide into two kinds. First, there are settings which are selected before shooting, and affect how the camera processes the image. Second, changes can be made to images already on the memory card; these changes don't alter the original photo but create a retouched copy.

It's particularly easy to get confused between the similarly-named Active D-Lighting (applied pre-shoot) and D-Lighting (applied post-shoot). D-Lighting, and other adjustments that can be applied to images already on the memory card, are gathered in the Retouch menu *(see page 107)*.

› Pre-shoot controls

We've already covered a range of settings which affect the qualities of the final image, such as exposure and white balance. The D3200 offers further options that can affect the look of the picture, principally Nikon Picture Controls and Active D-Lighting. However, these can only be accessed when shooting in P, S, A, or M modes. In Auto and Scene modes, Active D-Lighting is off and Picture Controls are preset *(see page 87)*.

Note:
These settings are useful for improving the quality of JPEG images. When shooting RAW files, they have no effect on the basic raw data. However, they can affect the appearance of the preview/playback image on the LCD screen, so it's helpful to make sure you're using appropriate settings for Picture Controls and Active D-Lighting.

› Active D-Lighting

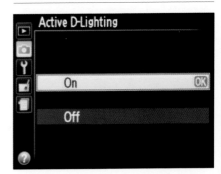

Setting Active D-Lighting in the Shooting menu

Active D-Lighting is designed to enhance the D3200's ability to cope with scenes that show a wide range of brightness (dynamic range). In simple terms, it reduces the overall exposure in order to capture more detail in the brightest areas, while mid-tones and shadows are

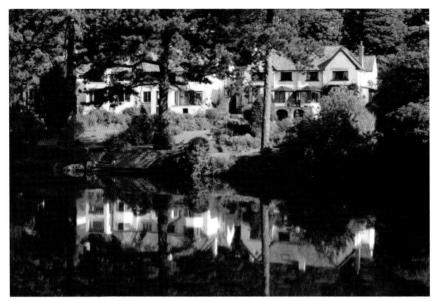

LIGHT AND SHADE ⌃
With brightly lit white walls and deep shadows in the same frame, this is just the sort of situation where Active D-Lighting scores. *42mm, 1/160 sec., f/10, ISO 200.*

subsequently lightened as the camera processes the image.

1) In the Shooting menu, select **Active D-Lighting**.

2) Select **Off** or **On** and press **OK**.

› Nikon Picture Controls

Picture Controls influence the way JPEG files are processed by the camera. In all modes the current Picture Control is indicated near top center of the Information Display. In Full Auto and Scene Modes the Picture Control is predetermined, but when shooting in P, S, A, or M modes you have a free hand to choose and fine-tune them.

The D3200 offers a selection of six preset Picture Controls. Names like

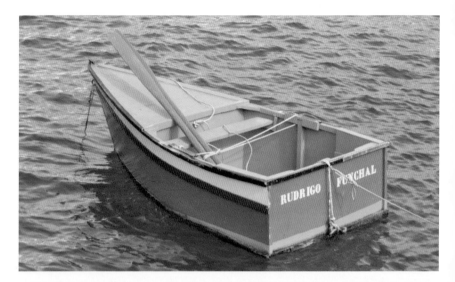

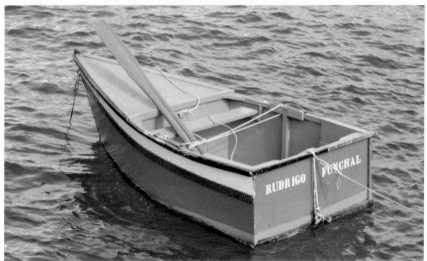

WATER COLOR
Neutral (top) and Vivid (bottom) Picture Controls applied to the same subject.

Neutral **(NL)** and **Vivid (VI)** are self-explanatory, and **Monochrome (MC)** even more so. **Standard (SD)** gives a compromise setting which works reasonably well in a wide range of situations. **Portrait (PT)** is designed to deliver slightly lower contrast and saturation, with color balance that is flattering to skin tones. **Landscape (LS)** produces higher contrast and saturation for more vibrant, punchy images.

Selecting Nikon Picture Controls

1) In the Shooting menu, select **Set Picture Control**.

2) Use the Multi-selector to highlight the required Picture Control and press **OK**. This Picture Control will apply to all images taken in P, S, A, or M modes until the setting is changed again. Scene modes continue to apply their preset Picture Controls.

Setting Picture Controls in the Shooting menu

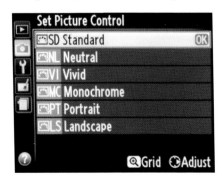

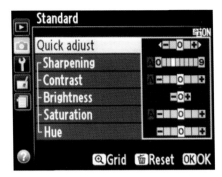

Modifying a Picture Control

Modifying Picture Controls

The standard Nikon Picture Controls can be modified. Use **Quick Adjust** to make swift global changes, or make manual adjustments to specific parameters (Sharpening, Contrast, and so on).

1) From the Shooting menu, select **Set Picture Control**.

2) Use the Multi-selector to highlight the required Picture Control and press ▶.

3) Scroll up or down with the Multi-selector to select **Quick Adjust** or one of the specific parameters. Use ▶ or ◀ to change the value as desired.

4) When all parameters are as required, press **OK**. The new values are retained (for images taken in P, S, A, or M modes) until that Picture Control is modified again, or you reset shooting menu *(see page 69).*

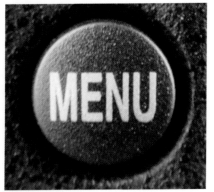

The **MENU** button

The options that you can access through buttons, Command Dial and Active Information Display are only the tip of the iceberg. There are many other ways in which you can customize the D3200 to suit you, but these are only revealed by delving into the menus. There are five of these: Playback menu, Shooting menu, Setup menu, Retouch menu and Recent Settings.

The Playback menu is underlined in blue and is used to control functions related to playback, including viewing, naming or deleting images. The Shooting menu is underlined in green and is used to control shooting settings, such as ISO speed or white balance (also accessible via the Active Information Display) as well as Picture Controls and Active D-Lighting. The Setup menu is underlined in orange

and is used for functions such as LCD brightness, plus others that you may touch rarely or never, such as language and time settings. The Retouch menu, underlined in purple, is used to create modified copies of images already on the memory card. Finally, Recent Settings is underlined in gray and allows fast access to recently used items from any of the other menus.

› Navigating the menus

1) To display the main menu screen, press **MENU**.

2) Scroll up or down with the Multi-selector to highlight the different menus. To enter the desired menu, press ▶ or **OK**.

3) Scroll up or down with the Multi-selector to highlight a menu item. To select an item, press ▶ or **OK**. This will take you to a further set of options.

4) Scroll up or down with the Multi-selector to choose the desired setting. To select, press ▶ or **OK**. In some cases it's necessary to select **DONE** and then press **OK** to make the changes effective.

5) To return to the previous screen, press ◀. To exit the menus completely without making any changes, semi-depress the shutter-release button.

» PLAYBACK MENU

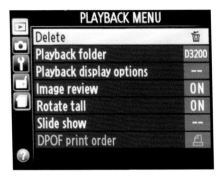

The D3200's Playback menu contains options which affect how images are viewed, stored, deleted and printed. It is only accessible when a memory card is present in the camera.

› Delete

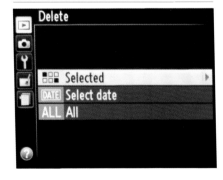

This function allows images stored on the memory card to be deleted, either singly or in batches.

1) In the Playback menu, highlight **Delete** and press ▶.

2) In the menu options screen, choose **Selected**. Images in the active playback folder or folders *(see page 92)* are displayed as thumbnail images.

3) Use the Multi-selector to scroll through the displayed images. Press and hold ⊕ to view the highlighted image full-screen. Press ⊕▣ to mark the highlighted shot for deletion. It will be tagged with a 🗑 icon. If you change your mind, highlight a tagged image and press ⊕▣ again to remove the tag.

4) Repeat this procedure to select further images. (To exit without deleting any images, press **MENU**.)

5) Press **OK** to see a confirmation screen. Select **YES** and press **OK** to delete the selected image(s); to exit without deleting any images, select **NO**.

> **Note:**
> Individual images can also be deleted when using the playback screen, and this is usually more convenient *(see page 85)*.

2

› Select date

Allows deletion of all images taken on a selected date.

1) In the Playback menu, highlight **Delete** and press ▶.

2) In the menu options screen, choose **Select date** and press ▶. A list of dates appears (corresponding to images on the memory card), with a sample image shown for each date. Scroll up or down to a desired date then press ▶ to select it.

3) Press **OK** again to delete all images taken on that date. Or, to review those images, press ◿▦ to see a screen of thumbnails. You can navigate through this in the usual way with the Multi-selector and press ◿ to see an image larger, but you can't zoom in any further. Press ◿▦ again to return to the date-selection screen.

4) With one or more dates checked, press **OK** to see a confirmation screen. Select **YES** and press **OK** to delete all image(s). To exit without deleting any images, select **NO**.

› All

1) To delete all images on a card (strictly, all images in the current folder—*see page 105*), highlight **Delete** and press ▶.

Note:
Deleting all images this way can take time and it is generally quicker to format the card instead *(see pages 28, 99)*. However, there is a significant difference. Delete all does not delete protected or hidden images, whereas formatting the card does remove these. (To protect images, exit the Playback menu and use the playback screen instead, *see page 85*.)

2) In the menu options screen, choose **All**.

3) Press **OK** to see a confirmation screen. Select **YES** and press **OK** to delete all image(s); to exit without deleting any images, select **NO**.

› Playback folder

Normally, the memory card stores all images in a single folder. However, you can create additional ones, and the camera will also create a new folder if the existing one reaches 999 images. The Setup menu is used to create new folders and select the current one *(see page 105)*.

By default, the D3200's playback screen only displays images in the current folder; if multiple folders exist, images in other folders will not be visible. You can use this menu to make all images visible.

Playback folder options

Current	Displays images in the current folder only.
All	Displays images in all folders on the memory card.

› Playback display options

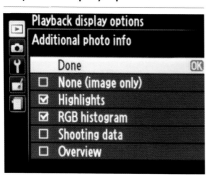

Playback display options, with Highlights and RGB histogram checked

This menu enables you to choose what information about each image will be available on playback. The "File information" page is always available, showing the image with basic data below and up to five additional screens can be enabled. For more *see page 82*.

> **Note:**
> To make checked options effective in this menu, you must scroll to **Done** at the top of the screen and then press **ON**.

Playback display options

Additional photo info	None (image only)	Full-screen image with no superimposed data
	Highlights	Areas of "blown" highlights are shown as black blinking areas in full-screen playback
	RGB histogram	Makes available a separate playback page with histograms for the three individual color channels
	Shooting data	Makes available three further playback pages containing detailed information about the image
	Overview	Shows small image, single histogram, and key shooting data
Transition effects	Slide in	Governs visual effect when scrolling from one image to the next
	Zoom/fade	
	None	

› Image review

If Image review is **ON**, (the default setting), images are automatically displayed on the monitor immediately after shooting. If **OFF**, this is not so and they can only be displayed by pressing ▶.

› Rotate tall

This enables you to determine whether portrait format ("tall") images will be displayed the "right way up" during playback. If set to **OFF**, these images will not be rotated, meaning that you need to turn the camera through 90° to view them correctly. If set to **ON**, these images will be displayed the right way up but, because the screen is rectangular, they will appear smaller. **ON** is useful when displaying images through a TV *(see page 239)*.

› Slide show

Enables you to display images as a standard slide show, on the camera's own screen or when connected to a TV. All the images in the folder or folders selected for playback (under the Playback folder menu) will be played in chronological order, but you can choose whether to include stills only, movies only, or both.

1) In the Playback menu, select **Slide show**.

2) Select **Image type** to decide whether the slide show will include **Still images and movies**, **Still images only**, or **Movies only**.

3) Select **Frame interval**. Choose between intervals of 2, 3, 5, or 10 seconds. Press **OK**. (This determines how long each still image will appear—it has no bearing on movies.)

4) Select **Transition effects** to change the appearance of the transition between stills. The options are **Zoom/fade**, **Cube**, and **None**.

5) Select Start and press **OK**.

6) When the show ends, a dialog screen is displayed. Select **Restart** and press **OK** to play again. You can also revisit **Frame interval** and **Transition effects**. Select Exit and press **OK** to exit.

7) If you press **OK** during the slide show, the slide show is paused and the same screen is displayed. The only difference is that if you select **Restart** and press **OK**, the show will resume where it left off.

8) To skip ahead, or skip back, while a slide show is playing, press ▶ or ◀ respectively.

9) To change display mode while a slide show is playing (e.g. to see a histogram for each image), press ▲ or ▼.

› DPOF print order

This allows you to select image(s) to be printed when the camera is connected to a suitable printer, i.e. one that complies with the DPOF (Digital Print Order Format) standard. DPOF print orders can also be saved on the memory card for later use, e.g. at a printing outlet. For more on printing generally *(see Chapter 9, page 230).*

Note:
NEF (RAW) images cannot be selected for printing by this method.

TOUCH OF FROST   ⩔

These maize cobs, picked out by the light of the just-risen sun on a frosty morning, have a real sculptural quality, and their color also contrasts beautifully with the bluer shadows on the earth around them. A white balance setting of Direct Sunlight *(see pages 63, 96)* helped keep colors true. *52mm, 1/160 sec., f/10, ISO 400.*

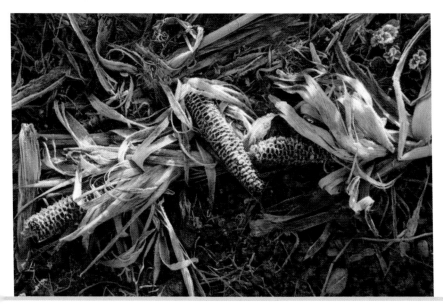

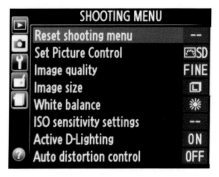

The Shooting menu contains numerous options, but many of these are also accessible through the Active Information Display and have already been discussed, so can be dealt with briefly here.

› Reset shooting options

Resets most options to default *(see pages 69 to 70)*.

› Set Picture Control

This menu governs the use of Nikon Picture Controls, as already discussed on *page 87*. **Set Picture Control** is only available in P, S, A and M exposure modes.

› Image quality

Use this to choose between RAW and JPEG options, as described on *page 61*.

› Image size

Use this to choose between Small, Medium and Large image sizes, as described on *page 62*.

> **Note:**
> If RAW or RAW+FINE is selected for Image Quality this Shooting menu item is grayed out and cannot be accessed.

› White balance

This menu allows you to set the white balance, as already discussed on *page 63*. It is only available in P, S, A, and M exposure modes.

› ISO sensitivity settings

This menu governs the ISO sensitivity setting, as already discussed on *page 67*.

› Active D-Lighting

This menu governs the use of Active D-Lighting, as already discussed on *page 86*. It is only available in P, S, A, and M exposure modes.

› Auto distortion control

If ON, this automatically corrects for distortion *(see page 138)* which may arise with certain lenses. It's available only with Type G and D lenses *(see page 198)*, excluding fisheye and perspective-control (PC) lenses, and only affects JPEG images.

› Color space

This menu allows you to choose between sRGB and Adobe RGB color spaces *(see page 68)*.

› Noise reduction

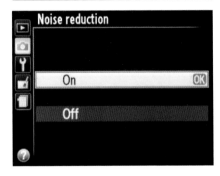

Photos taken at long shutter speeds and/or high ISO sensitivity settings can be subject to increased "noise" *(see page 141)* and the D3200 offers the option of extra image processing to counteract this. If noise reduction is **ON**, it applies at all ISO settings, but the difference is much more

obvious at higher settings. When noise reduction is applied at long shutter speeds, image processing takes a time roughly equal to the shutter speed in use. During this time, **Job nr** appears, blinking, in the viewfinder, and no further pictures can be taken until the processing is complete. This can obviously cause significant delays in shooting and it's often preferable to tackle image noise in post-processing instead. Because of this, the recommended setting is **OFF**, though a limited degree of noise reduction will still be applied to JPEG images shot at ISO 1600 or above.

› AF-area mode

Select the AF-area mode *(see page 56)*. AF-area mode is more usually chosen through the Active Information Display.

› Built-in AF-assist illuminator

Determine whether the AF-assist lamp operates in appropriate exposure modes *(see page 60)* or remains off in all modes.

› Metering

Select the metering pattern *(see page 49)*. Metering pattern is more usually chosen through the Active Information Display.

› Movie settings

Sets key options for movie shooting *(see page 183)*.

› Flash cntrl for built-in flash

Determine whether the output of the built-in flash is controlled automatically (**TTL**) or manually (**Manual**). Selecting Manual brings up a sub-menu which allows the strength of flash output to be set. For more on flash see Chapter 4 *(see page 150)*.

FALLING WATER ⌄

The built-in flash provides some extra sparkle in this long-exposure shot of a waterfall. 44mm, 4 sec., f/11, ISO 100.

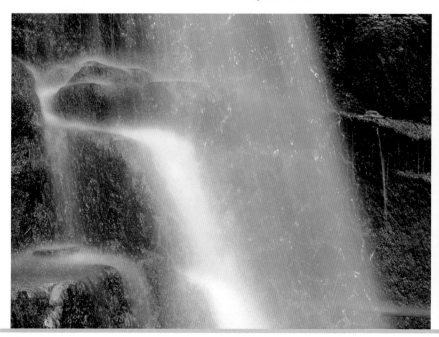

»› SETUP MENU

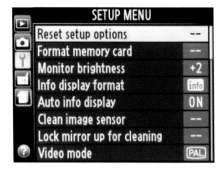

The Setup menu controls many important camera functions, though many are ones you will need to access only occasionally, if at all.

› Reset setup options

Resets most options in this menu to default *(see pages 69 to 70)*.

› Format memory card

The one item in this menu that most users will employ regularly *(see page 28)*.

› Monitor brightness

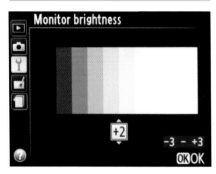

Allows the brightness of the LCD to be altered to suit ambient lighting conditions, using the Multi-selector.

› Info display format

Use this item to switch between two display modes for the Information Display: **Graphic** (the default) and **Classic** *(see page 32)*. You can also select different background colors for each display mode.

› Auto info display

This item determines whether the Information Display appears automatically when the shutter-release button is half-pressed. It can also be displayed straight after a shot is taken, but only if Image Review *(see page 94)* is **Off**.

› Clean image sensor

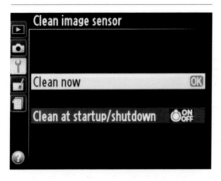

Strictly speaking, it's not the sensor itself but its protective low-pass filter that can attract dust and require cleaning. The D3200 has an automated procedure to do this, by vibrating the low-pass filter at various frequencies. Experience suggests that this is highly effective and greatly reduces both the incidence of dust spots on images and the need for more invasive forms of cleaning. The **Clean image sensor** menu allows you to actuate cleaning at any time, and also to set the camera to clean automatically at startup and/or shutdown.

› Lock mirror up for cleaning

Allows access to the low-pass filter for manual cleaning. For more details *see page 225*.

› Video mode

This is not directly related to the camera's Movie mode. You can connect the camera to a TV or VCR to view images. This menu sets the camera to **PAL** or **NTSC** standards to match the device you're connecting to. NTSC is used in North America and Japan, but most of the rest of the world uses PAL.

› HDMI

You can also connect the camera to HDMI (High Definition Multimedia Interface) TVs—you'll need a special cable. This menu sets the camera's output to match the HDMI device (get this information from that device's specs or instructions).

The **Device control** submenu applies when connected to an HDMI-CEC television, and allows the TV remote to be used to navigate through images.

› Flicker reduction

Some light sources (notably fluorescent lighting) can produce visible flicker in the Live View screen image and in movie recording. To minimize this, use this menu to match the frequency of the local mains power supply. 50Hz is normal in the European Union, including the UK, 60Hz is more common in North America.

› Time zone and date

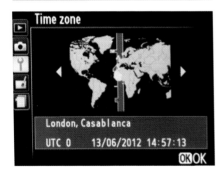

Allows you to set date, time and time zone, and to specify the format in which the date is displayed (**Y/M/D**, **M/D/Y**, or **D/M/Y**). It's best to set the time zone in which you normally operate first, then set the time correctly. Then, if you travel to a different

time zone, you need only change the time zone setting and the time will be corrected automatically.

› Language

Set the language which the camera uses in its menus. The options include most major European languages, Arabic, Indonesian, Chinese, Japanese, Korean, and Thai.

› Image comment

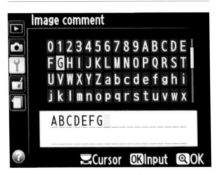

This allows you to add text comments to images as they are shot. Comments appear in the third page of the photo info display (when this is activated using **Display mode** in the Playback menu) and can also be viewed in Nikon View NX2 and Nikon Capture NX2.

The process of text input is similar to text-messaging on a mobile phone. To input a comment, select **Input comment** and press **OK**. Use the

2

Multi-selector to move through the available characters, and press **OK** to use the highlighted character. Use the Command Dial to move the cursor forward or back in the text. When finished press ⊕.

If you select **Attach comment**, select **Done** and press **OK**, the comment will be attached to all new shots until turned off again.

› Auto image rotation

If set to **ON** (default) information about the orientation of the camera is recorded with each photo taken, ensuring that they will appear the right way up when viewed with Nikon View NX2, Nikon Capture NX2 or most third-party imaging applications.

Exceptions can occur if shots are taken with the camera pointing steeply up or down, or when panning; in these cases orientation data may not be recorded. It might be worth setting Auto image rotation to **OFF** if a sequence of such shots is planned, but in practice there's little to be gained.

› Image Dust Off ref photo

Nikon Capture NX2 (not supplied with the camera, *see page 237*) features automatic removal of dust spots on images by comparing them with a reference photo which maps dust on the sensor. If you know there are stubborn dust spots that

don't succumb to the normal sensor cleaning, this can save a lot of grunt-work in Capture NX2 (or another imaging application).

To take a dust-off reference photo

1) Fit a CPU lens of at least 50mm focal length. If it's a zoom, use the longest setting. Locate a bright, featureless white object such as a sheet of plain paper, large enough to fill the frame.

2) In the Setup menu, select **Dust off ref photo** and press **OK**.

3) Select **Start** or **Clean sensor and then start** and press **OK**. (Do not select **Clean sensor and then start** if the pictures from which spots are to be removed have already been taken.)

4) When the camera is ready to shoot the reference photo, **rEF** appears in the viewfinder.

5) Frame the white object at a distance of approximately 4in. (10cm). Press the shutter-release button halfway; focus will automatically be set at infinity (in manual focus mode, set focus to infinity manually).

6) Press the shutter-release button fully to complete the process. If the reference object is too bright or dark, a warning will be displayed. Change exposure settings or choose another reference object and reshoot.

› Auto off timers

Governs the interval before the Information Display, playback display and viewfinder displays turn off if no further actions are carried out. A shorter delay is good for battery economy. **Short/Normal/Long** determine standard times for each of the three displays. **Custom** allows the user to set timings for each display individually.

> The meters will not turn off automatically when the D3200 is connected to a computer or printer, or powered by a mains adapter.

› Self-timer

Self-timer delay governs the delay in self-timer release mode *(see page 34)*. The options are 2, 5, 10 or 20 seconds.

> **Number of shots** allows multiple shots to be taken after the set delay, at 4-second intervals.

› Remote on duration

When using the optional ML-L3 remote control *(see page 220)*, this governs how long the camera will wait for a signal from the remote before reverting to normal shooting mode: 1, 5, 10 or 15 minutes.

› Beep

Governs the beep which sounds when the self-timer operates, and to signify that focus has been acquired when shooting in single-servo AF mode. Options are: **Off**, **High**, or **Low**. **High** and **Low** refer to pitch rather than volume.

› Rangefinder

If this setting is **On**, the electronic rangefinder can be used to assist with manual focusing *(see page 55)*.

› File number sequence

Controls how file numbers are set. If **Off**, file numbering is reset to 0001 whenever a memory card is inserted/formatted, or a new folder is created. If **On**, numbering continues from the previous highest number used. Reset creates a new folder and begins numbering from 0001.

› Buttons

This menu item has three sub-sections, which allow you to change the functions of three of the camera's control buttons *(see page 104)*.

2

Section	Options
Assign **Fn** button	**Image quality/size:** Press button and rotate Command Dial to scroll through full range of image quality/size options *(see page 61)*.
	ISO sensitivity: Press button and rotate Command Dial to select ISO setting *(see page 67)*.
	White balance (P, S, A or M modes only): Press button and rotate Command Dial to select white balance setting *(see page 63)*.
	Active D-Lighting (P, S, A or M modes only): Press button and rotate Command Dial to turn ADL On or Off *(see page 86)*.
Assign **AE-L/AF-L** button	**AE/AF lock** (default): Press and hold button to lock focus and exposure *(see page 52)*.
	AE lock only: Press and hold button to lock exposure *(see page 52)*.
	AF lock only: Press and hold button to lock focus *(see page 58)*.
	AE lock (hold): Press button to lock exposure *(see page 52)*.
	AF-ON: When AF-ON is selected, only the AE-L/AF-L button (not the shutter-release button) can be used to initiate autofocus.
Shutter-release button AE-L	**On:** Half-pressure on shutter-release button locks exposure and focus.
	Off (default): Half-pressure on shutter-release button locks focus only *(see page 58)*.

› Slot empty release lock

This menu item has two options. When **Release locked** (default) is selected, pictures cannot be taken if no memory card is inserted. If **Enable release** is selected, the shutter can be released even if no memory card is present. Images are held in the camera's buffer and can be displayed on the monitor (demo mode), but are not recorded.

› Print date

Governs whether date/time are imprinted on photos as they are taken. The default setting is **Off**. Other options allow imprint of Date, Date and time or Date counter, which imprints number of days to/from a selected date. Imprint applies to JPEG photos only.

› Storage folder

By default the D3200 stores images in a single folder (named 100D3200). If multiple memory cards are used they will all end up holding folders of the same name. This isn't usually a problem but a few users might wish to avoid it. You might also want to create specific folders for different shoots or different types of image. Generally, it's organizing images on the computer that counts *(see page 232)*, but having separate folders in the camera sometimes helps.

New folders are also created automatically if an existing folder becomes full. "Full" is defined as containing 999 photos, irrespective of image quality or size. If you regularly copy images to your computer and then format the memory card, which of course is recommended, the folder may never reach this capacity. However, a new folder will also be created when photo-numbering reaches 9999, and it is certainly possible to take more than 10,000 photos in the lifetime of a Nikon D3200.

In naming folders, you can't just use any name you like: only the last five digits of the name are editable. (In fact, the first three digits are hidden when you use this menu, but the full name appears when the camera is connected to a computer.)

To create a new folder

1) In the Shooting menu, select **Storage folder** and press **OK**.

2) Select **New** and press **OK**.

3) A screen of letters and numbers appears. Enter a new name (for text entry *see page 101*).

4) Press ⊕ to create the new folder and return to the Shooting menu. It automatically becomes the active folder. You can also rename an existing folder: at step 2 above select **Rename** and press **OK**; the procedure is then similar.

To change the active folder

This assumes that more than one folder already exists on the memory card in the camera.

1) In the Shooting menu, select **Storage folder** and press **OK**.

2) Select **Select folder** and press **OK**.

3) Scroll up or down the folder list. To select the highlighted folder press **OK**. To exit without making a change, press **MENU**.

2 › GPS

Used when the D3200 is connected to Nikon's GP-1 GPS device *(see page 221)*.

› Eye-Fi upload

Set up a WiFi network connection using an Eye-Fi card *(see page 235)*.

› Firmware version

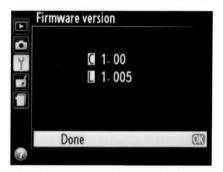

Firmware is the onboard software which controls the camera's operation. Nikon issues updates periodically. This menu shows the version presently installed, so you can verify whether it is current.

When new firmware is released, download it from the Nikon website and copy it to a memory card. Insert this card in the camera then use this menu to update the camera's firmware.

Note:
Firmware updates may include new functions and new menu items, which can render this Guide (and the Nikon manual) out of date.

›› RETOUCH MENU

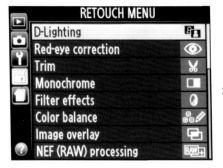

RETOUCH MENU
- D-Lighting
- Red-eye correction
- Trim
- Monochrome
- Filter effects
- Color balance
- Image overlay
- NEF (RAW) processing

The Retouch menu allows you to make various corrections and enhancements to images, including cropping, color balance and much more. Retouching does not overwrite the original image but creates a copy to which the changes are applied. Further retouching can be applied to the new copy, but you can't apply the same effect twice to the same image.

Copies are always created in JPEG format but the size and quality depends on the format of the original (a few exceptions, such as **Trim** and **Resize**, produce copies smaller than the original).

There are two ways to access the retouch options and create a copy: the steps of the process are basically the same, but in a slightly different sequence.

› From the Image Playback screen

1) Display the image you wish to retouch.

2) Press **OK** and the Retouch menu appears, overlaying the image.

3) Select the desired retouch option and press ▶. If subsidiary options appear, make a further selection and press ▶ again. A preview of the retouched image appears.

4) Depending on the type of retouching to be done (see details below), there may be further options to choose from.

5) Press **OK** to create a retouched copy. The access lamp will blink briefly as the copy is created. (◀ takes you back to the options screen and ▶ or **MENU** exits without creating the copy.)

› From the Retouch menu

1) In the Retouch menu, select the desired retouch option and press ▶. If subsidiary options appear, make a further selection and press ▶ again. A screen of image thumbnails appears.

Format of original photo	Quality and size of copy
NEF (RAW)	Fine, Large
JPEG	Quality and size match original

> **Note:**
> Retouched copy images are indicated by a 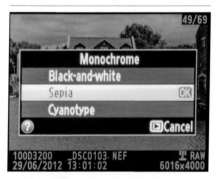 icon in normal image playback.

2) Select the required image using the Multi-selector, as you would during regular image playback. Press **OK**. A preview of the retouched image appears.

3) Depending on the type of retouching to be done *(see details below)*, there may be further options to choose from.

4) Press **OK** to create a retouched copy. The access lamp will blink briefly as the copy is created. (◄ takes you back to the options screen and ▶ or **MENU** exits without creating the copy.)

› Retouch menu options

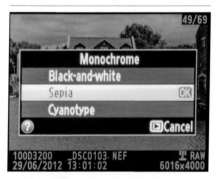

Applying a sepia effect in the Retouch menu, and the resulting image

D-Lighting

D-Lighting should not be confused with Active D-Lighting, though the end result is similar. Active D-Lighting *(see page 86)* is selected before shooting and affects the way the original image is exposed and processed; D-Lighting is applied after shooting and creates a retouched copy. Both effects aim to deal with high-contrast subjects and their primary effect is to lighten the shadow areas of the image. However, because it affects the original image exposure, Active D-Lighting is better at dealing with over-bright highlights.

The D-Lighting screen shows a side-by-side comparison of the original image and the retouched version; a press on ⊕ zooms in on the retouched version. Use ▲ and ▼ to select the strength of the effect—High, Normal or Low.

Red-eye correction

This is aimed at the notorious problem of "red-eye", caused by on-camera flash *(see page 158)*. This option can only be

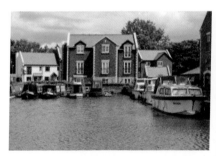

selected for photos which were taken using flash. The camera analyzes the photo for evidence of red-eye; if none is found the process will go no further. If red-eye is detected a preview image appears and you can use the Multi-selector and the zoom controls in the usual way to view it more closely. If you've used the zoom, a first press on **OK** returns to full-screen view and a second press on **OK** creates the retouched copy.

Trim

This allows you to crop an image to eliminate unwanted areas or to better fit it to a print size. When this option is selected, a preview screen appears, with the crop area shown by a yellow rectangle. Change the aspect ratio of the crop by rotating the Command Dial: choose from 3:2 (the same as the original image), 4:3, 5:4, 1:1 (square), and 16:9. Adjust the size of the cropped area using the ⊖▣ and ⊕ buttons. Adjust

its position using the Multi-selector. Press **OK** to save the cropped image as a copy.

Monochrome

This creates a monochrome copy of the original image. You can choose from straight **Black-and-white**, **Sepia** (a brownish-toned effect similar to many antique photos) and **Cyanotype** (a bluish-toned effect). If you select **Sepia** or **Cyanotype**, a preview screen appears and you can make the toning effect stronger or weaker with ◀ and ▲.

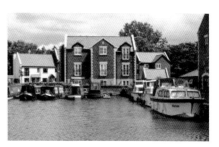

Cyanotype

Aspect ratio	Possible sizes for trimmed copy							
3:2	3840 x 2560	3200 x 2128	2560 x 1704	1920 x 1280	1280 x 856	960 x 640	640 x 424	
4:3	3840 x 2880	3840 x 2400	2560 x 1920	1920 x 1440	1280 x 960	960 x 720	640 x 480	
5:4	3600 x 2880	3008 x 2400	2400 x 1920	1808 x 1440	1200 x 960	896 x 720	608 x 480	
1:1	2880 x 2880	2400 x 2400	1920 x 1920	1440 x 1440	960 x 960	720 x 720	480 x 480	
16:9	4480 x 2520	3840 x 2160	3200 x 1800	2560 x 1440	1920 x 1080	1280 x 720	960 x 536	640 x 360

Filter option heading	Options available
Number of points	Create 4-, 6-, or 8-pointed star
Filter amount	Choose brightness of light sources that are affected
Filter angle	Choose angle of the star points
Length of points	Choose length of the star points
Confirm	See a preview of the effect; press $\oplus$ to see it full-screen
Save	Create a copy incorporating the effect

Filter effects

Mimics several common photographic filters (or perhaps we should say they used to be common in the days of film). **Skylight** reduces the blue cast which can affect photos taken on clear days with a lot of blue sky. Applied to other images its effect is very subtle, even undetectable. **Warm filter** has a much stronger warming effect. **Red**, **green** and **blue intensifier** are all fairly self-explanatory, as is **Soft**, but unlike **Cross screen**. This creates a "starburst" effect around light sources and other very bright points (like sparkling highlights on water).

There are multiple options within the **Cross screen** item.

Color balance

Creates a copy with modified color balance. When this option is selected a preview screen appears and the Multi-selector can be used to move a cursor around a color grid. The effect is shown both in the preview and in the histograms alongside.

Image overlay

Image overlay allows you to combine two existing photos into a new image. This can only be applied to originals in RAW format. Nikon claim (debatably) that the results are better than combining the images in applications like Photoshop because Image overlay makes direct use of the raw data from the camera's sensor.

This is the only Retouch menu item which allows you to create a new RAW image. You can also create JPEG images at any size and quality; the output will match the current Image Quality and Image Size options *(see pages 61, 62)*.

Creating an overlaid image

1) In the Retouch menu, select **Image overlay** and press **OK**. A dialog screen appears, with sections labeled **Image 1**, **Image 2** and **Preview**. Initially, **Image 1** is highlighted. Press **OK**.

2) The camera displays thumbnails of RAW images on the memory card. Select the first image you want to use for the overlay and press **OK**.

3) Select **Gain**: this determines how much "weight" this image has in the final overlay. Use ▲ and ◀ to adjust gain from a default value of 1.0.

4) Press ▶ to move to **Image 2**. Repeat steps 2 and 3 for the second image.

5) If necessary, press ◀ to return to Image 1. You can make further adjustments to Gain, or even press **OK** to change the selected image.

6) Finally, press ▶ to highlight **Preview**. Select **Overlay** and press **OK** to preview the overlay. If not satisfied you can return to the previous stage by pressing ◓▣. If you are satisfied, press **OK** again and the

overlay will be saved. You can also skip this preview stage by highlighting **Save** and pressing **OK**.

NEF (RAW) Processing

This menu creates JPEG copies from images originally shot as RAW files. While no substitute for full RAW processing on computer *(see page 232)* it allows the creation of quick copies for immediate sharing or printing. The screen shows a preview image, with processing options (see table below) in a column on the right. These do give considerable control over the resulting JPEG image.

When satisfied with the previewed image, select **EXE** and press **OK** to create the JPEG copy. Pressing ▶ or **MENU** exits without creating a copy.

Option	Description
Image quality	Choose Fine, Normal, or Basic *(see page 61)*.
Image size	Choose Large, Medium, or Small *(see page 62)*.
White balance	Choose a white balance setting; options are similar to those described *on page 64*.
Exposure comp.	Adjust exposure (brightness) levels from +2 to -2.
Set Picture Control	Choose any of the range of Nikon Picture Controls *(see page 87)* to be applied to the image.
High ISO NR	Choose whether or not to apply noise reduction *(see pages 97, 141)*.
Color space	Choose sRGB or Adobe RGB *(see page 68)*.
D-Lighting	Choose D-Lighting setting *(see page 108)*.

Option	Size (pixels)	Suitable display
2.5M	1920 x 1280	HD TV and larger computer monitor, latest iPad
1.1M	1280 x 856	Typical computer monitor, older iPads
0.6M	960 x 640	Standard (not HD) television, iPhone 4
0.3M	640 x 424	Mobile devices including older iPhones
0.1M	320 x 216	Standard mobile phone

Resize

This option creates a small copy of the selected picture(s), suitable for immediate use with various external devices. Five possible sizes are available *(see above)*.

Quick retouch

Provides basic one-step retouching for a quick fix, boosting saturation and contrast. D-Lighting is applied automatically to retain shadow detail. Use ▲ and ▼ to increase or reduce the strength of the effect, then press **OK** to create the retouched copy.

Straighten

It's best to get horizons level at the time of shooting, but it doesn't always happen. This option allows correction by up to 5° in steps of 0.25°. Use ▶ to rotate clockwise, ◀ to rotate anticlockwise. Inevitably, this crops the image slightly. As usual, press **OK** to create the retouched copy, press ▶ to exit without creating a copy.

Distortion control

Some lenses create noticeable curvature of straight lines *(see page 138)*—this menu allows you to correct this in-camera. This inevitably crops the image slightly. **Auto** allows automatic compensation for the known characteristics of Type G and D Nikkor lenses, but it can't be used on images taken with other lenses. **Manual** can be applied whatever lens was used—use ▶ to reduce barrel distortion, ◀ to reduce pincushion distortion. The Multi-selector can also be used for fine-tuning after **Auto** control is applied.

Fisheye

This is almost the reverse of the previous effect, applying exaggerated barrel distortion to give a fisheye lens effect. Use ▶ to strengthen the effect, ◀ to reduce it.

Color outline

This detects edges in the photograph and uses them to create a "line-drawing" effect. This could be used as a starting point for

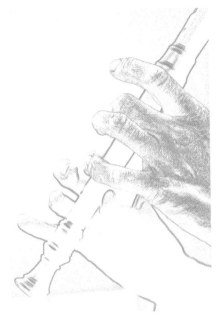

Color outline

Perspective control

Corrects the convergence of vertical lines in photos taken looking up, for example, at tall buildings. Grid lines aid in assessing the effect, and the strength of the effect is controlled with the Multi-selector. The process inevitably crops the original image, so it's vital to leave room around the subject when taking the original shot. For alternative approaches to perspective control, and an example, *see page 207*.

Miniature effect

This option mimics the technique, recently trendy for a short time, of shooting images with extremely small and localized depth of field *(see page 119)*, making real landscapes or city views look like miniature models. It usually works best with photos taken from a high viewpoint, which typically have clearer separation of foreground and background. A yellow rectangle shows the area which will remain in sharp focus. You can reposition and resize this using the Multi-selector. Press ⊕

painting or illustration, either by hand or using illustration software. There are no options for fine-tuning the effect in-camera.

Color sketch

Turns a photo into something resembling a colored pencil drawing. There are options for **Vividness** (changes strength of colors) and **Outlines** (makes lines thinner or thicker).

Color sketch *(for original see Lightroom screenshot on page 239)*.

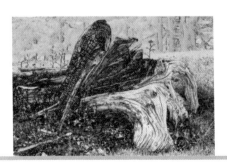

to preview the results and press **OK** to save a retouched copy.

Edit movie

This item has an inflated title; it merely allows you to trim the start and/or end of movie clips. It's a very long way from proper editing *(see page 190)*, but may have its uses when a clip is required straight away. There's also an option to extract a still frame as a JPEG image.

To trim a movie clip

1) Select a movie clip in full-frame playback. Press **OK** to play the movie.

2) Press ▼ to pause. If this is the point at which you want to trim the movie, go to the next step. Otherwise press **OK** to resume playback or ◄ to rewind.

3) Press **AE-L/AF-L** to display the **Edit movie** options.

4) Select **Choose start/end point** and press ▶. Select **Choose start point** or **Choose end point** as required then press **OK** to trim the clip at this point.

5) Repeat if necessary to trim the other end of the clip.

6) Select **Save as new file** and press **OK** to save the trimmed clip as a copy (the original is retained). Or select **Overwrite existing file** and press **OK** to save the trimmed clip as a replacement for the

original: there's no going back, so exercize this option with caution.

To extract a still frame

Follow the above to Step 4 then select **Save selected frame** and press **OK**. The still frame is saved as a JPEG; image size is the same as the movie frame size, i.e. the maximum is 1920 x 1280 pixels, considerably smaller than regular still images (even Small JPEG images are 3008 x 2000).

> ### Tip
>
> *If you need full-size still photos to accompany a movie shoot, you need to take them there and then. See page 184 for how to do this.*

Side-by-side comparison

This is only available when a retouched copy, or its source image, is selected. Press **OK** in full-frame playback. You can't access this option from the Retouch menu. It displays the copy alongside the original source image. Highlight either image and press ⊕ to view it full frame. Press ▶ to return to normal playback; to return to the main playback screen, press **OK**.

› RECENT SETTINGS MENU

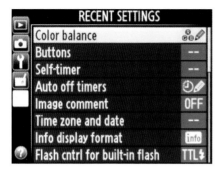

The Recent Settings menu automatically stores the most recent settings (up to 20 items) made using any of the other menus, and provides a quick way to access controls that you have used recently. It is possible to delete items from the list. This can be useful, for example, if you've recently made extensive use of the Retouch menu. By deleting the Retouch options from the Recent settings list you bring shooting settings—which are usually more useful— back to the top of the list.

To remove items from the Recent settings menu:

1) Highlight any item in the list and press 🗑 to select it for deletion. A confirmation dialog appears.

2) To go ahead with the deletion(s) press 🗑 again. To exit without deleting anything, press **MENU**.

> **Note:**
> Even if you start with a "full" Recent settings menu (20 items), deleting items simply makes the list shorter. The camera does not "recall" older items.

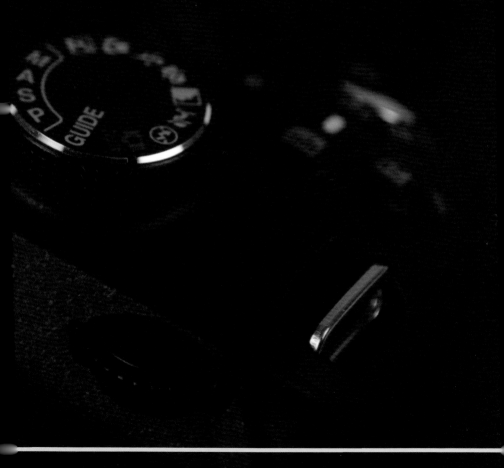

Chapter 3
IN THE FIELD

3 IN THE FIELD

Cameras like the D3200 are so capable that getting focusing and exposure right is rarely a major worry. However, there's a big difference between photos that "come out" and those that turn out exactly the way you want them. A fundamental thing to remember—and this is true of all cameras—is that the camera does not simply record what you see. We could call this the "point and shoot fallacy'. Cameras, lenses and digital image sensors do not work in the same way as the human eye and brain.

Take motion, for example: we see movement but the camera records a still image. Once we understand that cameras see differently, we can make it a strength, not a weakness. Many of the best photographs work precisely because they don't just mimic what the unaided eye sees. There are no "point and shoot" cameras, only "point and shoot" photographers.

Understanding how light works, and how lenses and digital images behave all make it easier to take charge and realize your own vision. However, the D3200 does not force you to dive in at the deep end and master all these things at once. Exploring the Guide mode and experimenting with Scene modes is a good way to start. Try shooting the same subject using different modes to see how different the results can be. Program mode leaves the camera in charge of the key shooting parameters, aperture and shutter speed, while allowing you to make choices over other important settings such as White Balance, Picture Controls or Active D-Lighting. Aperture-priority and Shutter-priority modes give control over these vital parameters but still allow the camera to determine correct exposure.

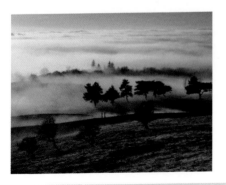

MIST OPPORTUNITY «
Camera skills are important, but there's still no substitute for being in the right place at the right time. *34mm, 1/640 sec., f/13, ISO 200.*

·› DEPTH OF FIELD

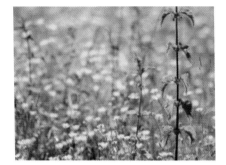
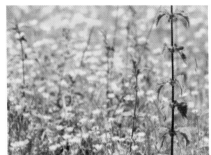

No camera, however sophisticated, always see what the eye sees. Nothing illustrates this better than depth of field. In simple terms, depth of field means what's in focus and what isn't. A more precise definition is: *depth of field is the zone, extending in front of and behind the point of focus, in which objects appear to be sharp in the final image.*

The eye scans the world dynamically; whatever we're looking at, near or far, normally appears in focus. (At least, it does if you have good eyesight, or appropriate glasses or contact lenses!) This gives us a sense that everything is in focus, which photographs often fail to match.

In landscape photography it's traditional to try and match this "all-in-focus" view of the world, by trying to ensure that depth of field covers everything in the frame. However, we can always choose to take a different

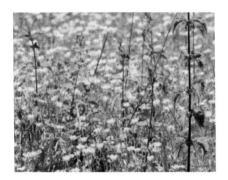

TEST OF NETTLE ⌃
The same setup, focused on the nettle on the right, taken at f/4, f/11 and f/32, shows the effect on depth of field. *300mm, varying shutter speed, ISO 200.*

approach; we can take photos with much narrower depth of field as a deliberate creative choice or simply because it's the only practical option.

Three main factors determine depth of

3

field: the focal length of the lens, the aperture, and the distance to the subject. Both focal length and subject distance are often determined by other factors, so aperture is key. The simple rule is: small aperture = big depth of field, and vice versa.

Depth of field preview

When you look through the viewfinder, the lens is set at its widest aperture; if a smaller aperture is selected, the lens stops down at the moment the picture is actually taken. This makes the viewfinder image an unreliable guide to the depth of field in the final shot. Many Nikon DSLRs, but not the D3200, have a depth of field preview button. This stops the lens down to the selected aperture, but unfortunately it also darkens the image and assessing sharpness isn't always easy.

Fortunately, there are alternatives. One is by using Live View. When you enter Live View, the camera stops down to the currently set aperture. However, it doesn't readjust if you change the aperture setting with the Command Dial. It will only reset the aperture if you exit and resume Live View (or take a picture). Still, this is a useful benefit of Live View on the D3200.

You can also get a sense of the depth of field by taking a test shot and reviewing it on the monitor. Both Live View and image review allow you to zoom in for a closer look. If you take time to use them, both can give you more information than the depth of field preview button ever did.

Hyperfocal distance

When you really need an image to be sharp from front to back, where should you focus? Focusing on the most distant object wastes all the depth of field

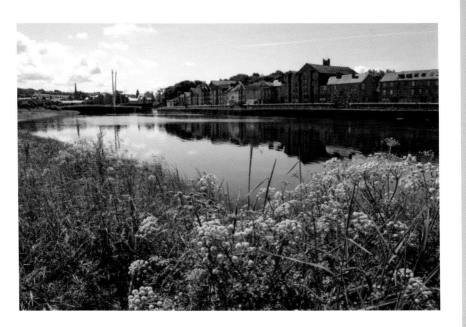

beyond it; focusing on the closest object equally wastes depth of field in front of it. Clearly you should focus in-between—but where, exactly?

If you need depth of field to extend right out to "infinity" (in practical terms, anything at a great distance), the answer is what's called the hyperfocal distance. This is not fixed, but varies with focal length and aperture. You can get tables and calculators to work it out, but usually this is overkill.

In an attempt to simplify things, you'll often see advice to "focus one third of the way into the picture". Unfortunately, this is meaningless: what's one third of the way to

HYPERFOCAL FLOWERS ⌃
I wanted both the nearest flowers and the distant cityscape to be sharp, and focusing at the hyperfocal distance helped make it so. In practice this meant focusing on the clump of plants left of center and at mid-height in the frame. *18mm, 1/320 sec., f/11, ISO 200.*

infinity? Sometimes, focusing about a third of the way up from the bottom of the picture works quite well, but only when the shot is very conventionally framed. An alternative way of putting it, which seems at least equally helpful, is to "focus at the far end of the foreground". Or, simpler still: the hyperfocal point is closer than you think.

In any case, it's not always possible to guarantee depth of field stretching from your toes to the horizon. Sometimes you'll have to compromise. An out-of-focus foreground usually looks less natural and more distracting than a bit of softness in the far distance, so it's usually better to err on the nearer side in focusing.

Apparent sharpness

Details may appear to be sharp in a small print or a web image but start to look fuzzy when the image is enlarged. "Pixel-peeping" at 100% magnification on your computer screen will often reveal a bit of softness in some areas, yet they can appear perfectly sharp when viewing the image as a whole or in a moderate-size print.

Depth of field is really a relative value rather than an absolute. It's easy to forget this and become obsessive about always using the smallest apertures and determining the hyperfocal distance. This may be overkill unless you are planning to make big prints or submit your images for magazine reproduction. A couple of presses on the ⊕ button is sufficient to check sharpness and depth of field for images which will be printed small or viewed on-screen.

Tips

If you are interested in determining the hyperfocal distance precisely, and don't have a calculator to hand, try this: focus on infinity (in practice, the most distant object in the scene). Playback the image and locate the nearest object which appears sharp: this is at the hyperfocal distance. Refocus on this object/at this distance for maximum depth of field.

While depth of field is very important, and hyperfocal distance is a useful concept, it's easy to become obsessive about it, and always using the smallest apertures. This may be overkill unless you plan to make big prints or submit images for magazine reproduction. There's much more tolerance in images which will be used at smaller sizes. And remember, not every image has to have maximum depth of field anyway. Sometimes shallow depth of field is exactly what you want.

Perspective-control lenses (see page 207) give much more precise control over depth of field, and can deliver far greater depth of field than "normal" lenses.

» PHOTOGRAPHING MOTION

Of course the D3200 is a capable video camera, but still images can also convey movement extremely well. However, this is a classic example of the camera not seeing what the eye sees: we see movement, but the camera produces still images.

This isn't necessarily a drawback: it often reveals drama and grace that may be missed with the naked eye.

Freezing the action

Dynamic posture and straining muscles shout "movement"; the pin-sharp definition delivered by a fast shutter speed can enhance this impression. But what does "fast" mean? Should you set the D3200's maximum 1/4000 sec. every time?

The answer to the second is definitely "No", but the first is harder to resolve. The exact shutter speed needed to capture a sharp, frozen image depends on various factors: not just the speed of the subject, but its size and distance. It can be easier to get a sharp image of a train traveling at 200mph than of a cyclist doing 30, because you need to shoot from much closer range. The direction of movement is another factor: subjects passing across the frame need faster shutter speeds than those moving towards or away from the camera.

CATCHING THE BOAT   ⌄
A fast shutter speed freezes every element of the image, but there's still a strong sense of speed with this pilot boat. *200mm, 1/640 sec., f/8, ISO 200.*

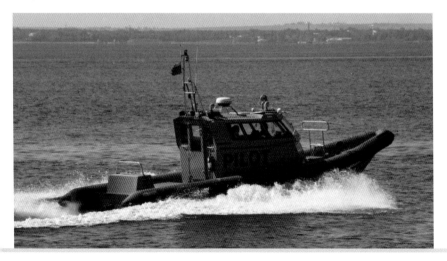

There's no "right" shutter speed, but you can play safe by setting the fastest shutter speed possible under the prevailing light conditions, as the D3200's Sports mode does. For more control, Shutter-priority is the obvious exposure mode to use.

Check images on the monitor whenever possible, and if a faster shutter speed appears necessary, be prepared to increase the ISO setting *(see page 67)*. If you shoot a particular activity on a regular basis, you'll soon discover what works for your particular needs.

Panning

With subjects moving across the field of view, panning is an excellent way to convey a sense of movement. By following the subject with the camera, it is recorded relatively sharply while the background becomes a streaky blur. The exact effect varies, so it's worth experimenting, especially before a critical shoot. Panning usually requires relatively slow shutter speeds: anything from 1/8–1/125 sec. can work and you may even go outside this range. Faster shutter speeds diminish background blur but give a sharper main subject. Sports mode is no use for this; use Shutter-priority or Manual.

Panning is usually easiest with a standard or short telephoto lens, but the choice is often dictated by working distance (e.g. behind barriers at sports events). Maintain a smooth panning movement during the

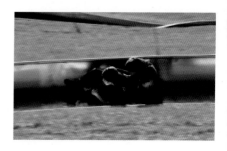

SLIDE VIEW ⏶
A classic panning shot, with regular movement across the field of view. *200mm, 1/160 sec., f/10, ISO 200.*

exposure; keep following through even after pressing the shutter.

Blur

Blur can also imply movement. It may be a necessity, because you just can't set a fast enough shutter speed, or it may be a creative choice, like the silky effect achieved by shooting waterfalls at exposures measured in seconds rather than fractions.

To ensure that only the moving elements are blurred, secure the camera on a tripod or other solid support, but you can also try for a more impressionistic effect by handholding. Again, Sports mode

---

Tip

When you want to embrace creative blur, turn Vibration Reduction OFF on VR lenses.

FLASH PAST »
A discreet amount of fill-in flash sharpens up the rider. *50mm, 1/50 sec., f/5.6, ISO 400.*

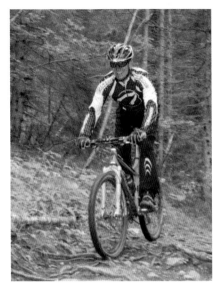

is no help and Shutter-priority is the obvious choice.

Camera shake

Camera shake can produce anything from marginal loss of sharpness to a hopeless mish-mash. Careful handling and the use of a camera support *(see page 222)* or Vibration Reduction (VR) lenses *(see page 199)* alleviate it.

FALLING WATER ⌄
A slow shutter speed smoothed the water and a tripod ensured the rocks and vegetation are sharp. *72mm, 2 sec., f/25, ISO 100.*

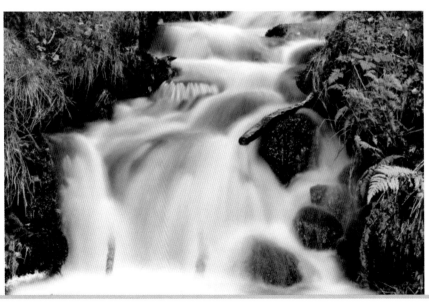

3 » COMPOSITION

Composition is a small word but a big subject. Composition, understood in its widest sense, is why some photos are perfectly exposed and focused but visually or emotionally dull, while others can be heart-stopping even if technically flawed. Composition is where to shoot from, where to aim the camera, how wide a view you want, what to include and what to leave out. All of these come before and stand above any so-called "rules of composition". Get these things right and you'll probably do pretty well without worrying about "rules": ignore them and "rules" won't help you anyway.

The essence of composition is simple (though not necessarily easy). Taking a photograph means selecting some part of our boundless, three-dimensional world and turning it into a two-dimensional rectangle. Most of the time, apart from perhaps when we look out of a window, we don't really see the world in rectangles. But we're very happy to confine it this way in photographs (not to mention the vast majority of paintings and drawings).

BREAKING DOWN FENCES ⌄
Framing is about seeing a picture as a complete entity. *26mm, 1/500 sec., f/13, ISO 200.*

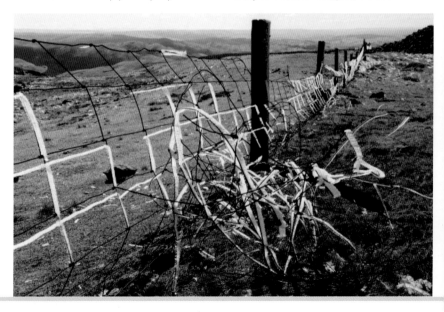

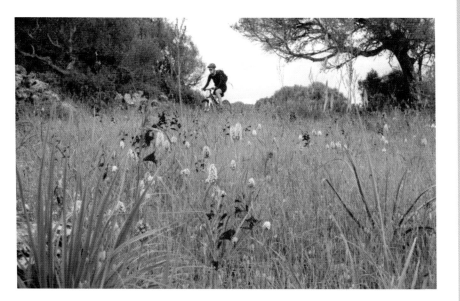

FIELD OF VIEW ⌃
There's no single "subject" in this image. *25mm, 1/160 sec., f/7.1, ISO 400.*

When we really think about photographs as rectangles, we should start to become very aware of edges—both the edges of the viewfinder/screen and the edges of the picture itself. They're key to what's included and what's left out. Our eyes and brains can "zoom in" selectively on the interesting bits of a scene, but the camera will happily and indiscriminately record all sorts of bits that we didn't even notice. This, all too often, produces pictures that seem cluttered or confusing. So it's important to see what the camera sees, not just what we want to see.

Looking through a traditional viewfinder is rather like looking through a window. In Live View mode, on the other

hand, you're very obviously looking at a screen. One immediate difference is that the screen image is more obviously two-dimensional—like a picture. Perhaps there are subtler differences too; intuition

> ### *Tip*
>
> *The great Ansel Adams said many wise things about photography, and none were wiser than this: "There are no rules for good photographs, there are only good photographs."*

3

and wobbly, drains batteries and becomes unclear in bright sunlight. The viewfinder is superior for most shooting, but the "Live View-Picture" approach is a worthwhile exercise. When you revert to the viewfinder, make a conscious effort to see it as a picture: look at the whole image, take note of the edges and what's included, and consciously seek out distracting and irrelevant elements.

Framing the landscape

We mentioned that a key part of framing is what to include and what to leave out.

suggests that using the screen to frame a shot might make it easier to see the whole image—the bits you're interested in and the bits you aren't interested in.

Using the screen continuously isn't recommended. It makes handling awkward

UPHILL AND DOWN DALE ⌄
A wide-angle lens can integrate foreground interest and the broad sweep of a landscape. *12mm, 1/200 sec., f/11, ISO 160.*

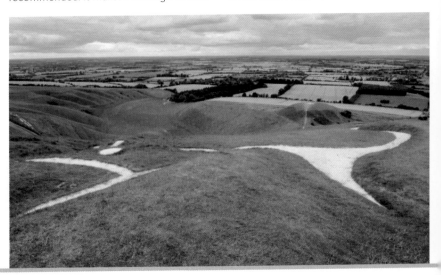

With some shots this seems relatively simple—we know what the subject is. It could be a portrait shot of a person, an action shot of an athlete, a close-up of a flower. There are still decisions to be made—such as what sort of background you want—but at least we know what the photo is primarily about. Landscape photography is different.

Generally, landscapes don't offer up neat, predefined "subjects". You have to start by deciding which bit or bits of the landscape you want to photograph. There are no right and wrong ways to do this: a lot of it is about how you feel and how you react to the landscape. However, there are a few principles that can be helpful.

One of the most useful is to think about the foreground. After all, the foreground is where you're standing, and it's the start of your connection to the landscape. Foregrounds also show texture and detail, which imply sound, smell and touch (and sometimes even taste!) Foregrounds are our friends—never more so than when the distant scene is hazy or flatly-lit and long-range shots just look dull. Foregrounds can also help to convey depth and distance, and strengthen a sense of scale. Strong foregrounds are usually close foregrounds. Get close, and don't be afraid to exploit the third dimension: sit, kneel, crawl, climb.

To unite a strong foreground and a broad vista usually requires a wide-angle lens. The D3200 has a 1.5x magnification

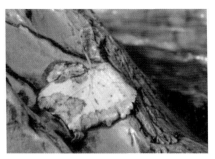

STREAM OF CONSCIOUSNESS ⌃
Small details can say a lot about a place, but this shot is not solely an image of a leaf. The detail in the rocks and the river flowing behind are also significant. *50mm, 1/50 sec., f/11, ISO 400.*

factor, so that a typical wide-angle zoom, with a minimum focal length of 18mm, gives the same coverage as a 27mm lens would on a 35mm SLR or a "full-frame" digital SLR like the D4. If you want to make the most of foregrounds, or big vistas, you'll soon hanker after something wider, like the Nikkor 12–24mm f/4G *(see page 208)*.

Not every landscape is on the grand scale. Small details can also convey the essence of a place. And if the light is not magical, if distant prospects look flat or hazy, details and textures and the miniature landscapes of a rockpool or forest clearing can bring the pictures back to life. Variations in scale, focus and so on also help liven up sequences of pictures. However good they are individually, an unrelieved sequence of big landscape images will eventually become oppressive.

3 » LIGHTING

Light is our raw material. Without light there are no photos. And because it's universal, we can easily take it for granted—"let the camera take care of it". However, it really is worth being aware of light in all its variety. It's rewarding in itself, and it generally leads to better pictures.

Infinite variety

Light varies in many ways: intensity, color, direction, whether it's "hard" or "soft." All of these qualities have an impact in photographs. Intensity—whether it's bright or dim—is perhaps the most obvious, and we've already looked at

ways of responding to this like exposure, metering and ISO settings.

Light sources

Natural light essentially means sunlight—direct or indirect. Even moonlight is reflected sunlight. The sun itself varies little, but by the time it reaches the camera its light can be modified in many ways by

PICTURE PERFECT ⌄
All sorts of factors can make the light more interesting; here it's the clouds, both those covering the distant hills and the unseen ones whose shadows add drama to the foreground. *18mm, 1/320 sec., f/11, ISO 200.*

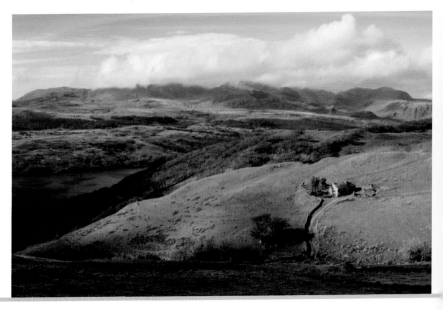

the Earth's atmosphere and by reflection. As a direct light source, the sun is very small, giving strongly directional light and hard-edged shadows, yet on an overcast day the same light can be spread across the entire sky, giving a soft even light. Studio photographers use massive "softboxes" to replicate this effect; the closest the average user can get, on a small scale, is usually with bounce flash *(see page 161)*.

Beyond sun and flash there are many other artificial light sources, and their color can vary enormously—making the D3200's White Balance controls invaluable—but other qualities, like direction and contrast, can usually be understood by comparison with more familiar sunlight and flash.

Contrast and dynamic range

Contrast, dynamic range, tonal range: these terms all refer to the range of brightness between the brightest and darkest areas of a scene or subject. Just as our eyes adjust focus dynamically to create what seems like vast depth of field, they also adapt rapidly to let us see detail in both bright areas and deep shade. Even the best cameras often fall short by comparison when contrast is high.

A typical example is when the sun shines from a clear sky—contrast may be even higher in deserts and at high altitude. In these "hard" lighting conditions bright highlights, like white clouds or snow, may appear completely blank and white, or the deepest shadows turn dead black, or even both together. This is often called "clipping." Even without clipping, hard light can produce hard shadows, which aren't ideal for every subject; they tend to be unflattering in portraits, for example.

In overcast, "soft", lighting conditions, contrast is much lower. This is much easier for the camera to deal with but can still produce great images of suitable subjects, such as portraits and flower studies.

High contrast, with its risk of clipping, is more challenging, but the D3200 offers several possible approaches. For closer subjects, like portraits, you can compensate by throwing some light back into the shadows, either using fill-in flash *(see page 152)* or a reflector. At longer range this is not an option, but Active D-Lighting or D-Lighting *(see pages 86, 108)* can help. Shooting RAW images also gives a chance of recovering highlight and/or shadow detail in postprocessing. However, all these

Tip

Even if the highlights display shows clipping, some highlight detail may be recoverable when shooting RAW. However, it may still be worth bracketing exposures (see page 52) for insurance.

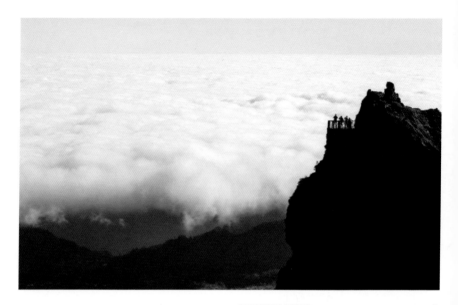

have their limits. Sometimes it's just not possible to capture the entire brightness range of a scene in a single exposure. The histogram display and the highlights display *(see page 83)* help you to see when this is happening, and how large an area is affected. Digital imaging also offers

PEAK PRACTICE ⌃
High dynamic range poses a challenge for any photographer, but it crops up in many of the shots we're most likely to want to take. *72mm, 1/320 sec., f/13, ISO 200.*

another solution. This involves making making multiple bracketed *(see page 52)* exposures—typically one for the bright areas, one that's right for the mid-tones and another for the shadows—which can be combined on the computer later. A solid tripod is essential to keep the images aligned, but this approach can become unusable when there's movement in the scene.

Tip

High dynamic range (HDR) software is specifically designed to facilitate the merging of images which cover a wide dynamic range. Adobe Photoshop (from CS3 onwards) has HDR capabilities.

Direction of light

And then there's the question of where the light is coming from: in front, behind, from the side?

Frontal lighting is what you get with on-camera flash, or with the sun behind you. It hits head-on, drenching everything with light, leaving few visible shadows. The resulting photos often look flat and uniform, but it can work well with images that rely on pure color, shape, or pattern. True frontal lighting doesn't lead to extremes of contrast, so exposure is usually straightforward.

Side lighting is more complex and

usually more interesting, with shadows defining forms and textures. At really acute angles, the light accentuates fine details, from crystals in rock to individual blades of grass. This is one reason why dedicated landscape photographers love the beginning and end of the day. However, in hillier terrain, even a high sun may still cast useful shadows. In some places, such as deep gorges, direct light only penetrates when the sun's high. Side lighting is terrific

SEEING THE LIGHT   «
These three shots of the same subject show frontal, oblique and back-lighting respectively. *100mm, 1/2 sec., f/11, ISO 200.*

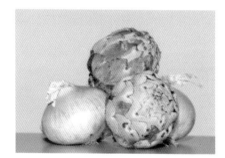

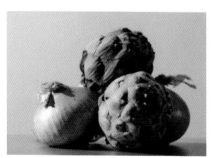

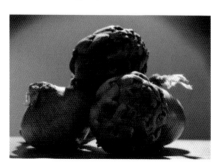

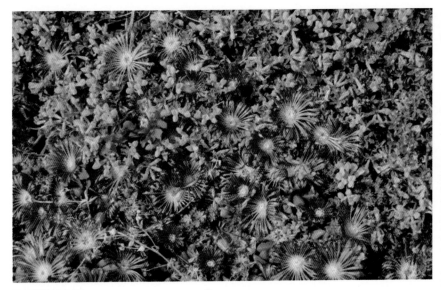

FLOWER SHOW ⌃
Frontal lighting works well with strong shapes and colors. *70mm, 1/400 sec., f/11, ISO 200.*

for landscapes, and many other subjects, but often goes hand in hand with high contrast. Backlighting can give striking and beautiful results, but handle with care. Translucent materials like foliage and fabric can glow beautifully when backlit, but more solid subjects can appear as mere silhouettes—this may be ideal: bare trees can look fantastic against a colourful sky. When you don't want a silhouette effect, a reflector or fill-in flash can help. You can also add some exposure compensation *(see page 50)* to lighten the subject, but this will weaken the background too.

Color

Light comes in many colors, but most of the time we barely notice; instead we see, or think we see, the colors of things. Cameras, however, are more observant. Most of the time, Auto White Balance will take account of changing light and keep colors looking pretty natural, but there are times when it may stumble (especially under artificial light).

The warmer light of a low sun is one reason why landscape photographers traditionally favor mornings and evenings. It's not just that that we tend to find warm colors more pleasing; if that was all, the effect could be easily replicated with a Photoshop adjustment. In the real world,

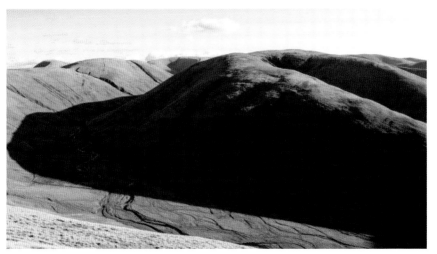

SLOPE SHADOW ⌃
Oblique lighting emphasizes the forms of the hills. *18mm, 1/25 sec., f/11, ISO 100.*

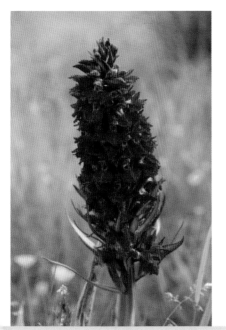

however, sunlit surfaces pick up a warm hue, while shadows receive light from the sky, tinting them blue. While most obvious in snow scenes, it's almost always true.

This difference in color between sunlit and shadow areas increases as the direct sunlight becomes redder, adding vibrancy to morning and evening shots. Filters can't duplicate this effect. When shifting colors are part of the attraction, you don't want to neutralize or "correct" them back to "normal." However, if white balance is set

SOFT ORCHID «
Soft light also works well with strong shapes and colors, and keeps contrast within manageable limits. *55mm, 1/200 sec., f/8, ISO 200.*

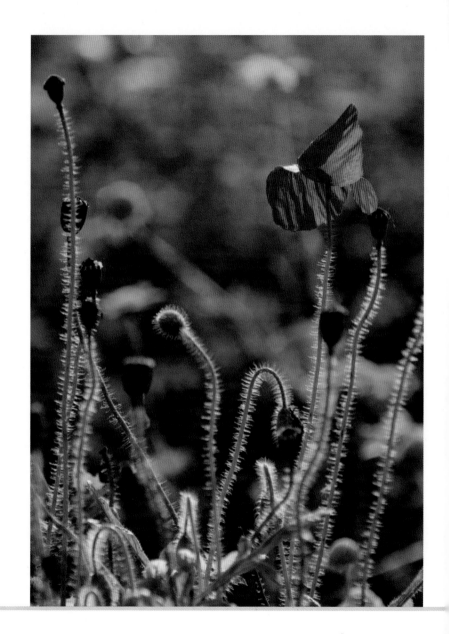

to **Auto** (as it is in Full Auto and Scene Modes), the D3200 may attempt to do exactly this. Try shooting in one of the user-control modes and changing the white balance setting to **Direct sunlight** instead. Similar principles apply with artificial light. Sometimes you'll want to correct its color, sometimes it's better left alone. Portraits shot under fluorescent lamps can take on a ghastly greenish hue. Auto White Balance often improves matters, but isn't always perfect under artificial light. On the other hand, if you're shooting floodlit buildings, the variations in color may be part of the appeal.

POPPY SHOT «
Backlighting makes many subjects appear luminous. *300mm, 1/1000 sec., f/6.3, ISO 200.*

Tip

Shooting RAW gives you far more scope for adjusting the white balance later. Another option, when shooting JPEGs, is to take several shots at different WB settings: white balance bracketing, in fact.

Understanding light and what it's doing is important, but don't get too hung up on it. Never let the "wrong" light get in the way of taking a shot: if it looks good to you, go for it.

TREE ⌄
The warm light contrasts with the cool shadows. *38mm, 1/125 sec., f/10, ISO 400.*

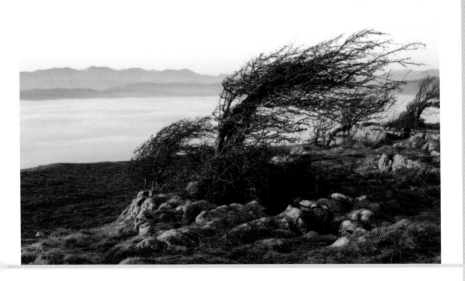

3 » IMAGE PROPERTIES—OPTICAL

There are still more ways in which what the camera sees doesn't match what the eye sees. Some of these arise from the fact that camera lenses are very different from the human eye.

Flare

Lens flare results from stray light bouncing around within the lens. It usually occurs when shooting towards the sun, whether the sun is actually in frame or just outside. It may produce a string of colored blobs, apparently radiating from the sun, or a more general veiling effect. You'll usually be able to see it in the viewfinder or on the LCD screen, but check again on playback.

If the sun's actually in frame, you can sometimes mask it, perhaps behind a tree. If it's not in shot, try to shield the lens. You can use a piece of card, a map, or your hand. This is easiest with the camera on a tripod; otherwise it requires one-handed

shooting (or a friend). Check playback carefully. Because the viewfinder does not quite show 100% of the image, watch out for that map/card/hand creeping into shot!

Distortion

Distortion means that straight lines appear in the image as curves. When straight lines bow outwards, it's called barrel distortion; when they bend inwards it's pincushion distortion.

Both problems can be forestalled using Auto Distortion Control (Shooting menu)—if you're using a Type G or D lens. They can also be corrected using Distortion Control in the Retouch menu, or in later processing with software such as Nikon Capture NX2 or Adobe Photoshop. However, all these methods crop the

FLARE FIGHT ⌄
Flare is all too obvious in the first shot but was eliminated by shading the lens. *14mm, 1/80 sec., f/10, ISO 200.*

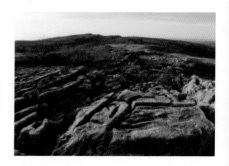

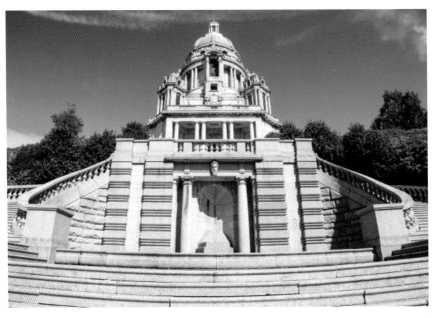

STEP AROUND ⌃
Converging verticals were inevitable in this shot looking steeply up at this memorial. But the curvature of the nearby steps is blatant barrel distortion (note: added in post-processing—I don't own any lenses that are this bad!) *13mm, 1/250 sec., f/7.1, ISO 100.*

image, and it's better to avoid the issue in the first place by using good lenses.

Distortion may go unnoticed when shooting natural subjects with no straight lines, but it can still rear its ugly head when a level horizon appears in a landscape or seascape, especially when that horizon is near the top or bottom of the frame.

Aberration

Aberration is a lens property which occurs when light rays from the subject aren't all

focused together. Chromatic aberration occurs when light of different colors is focused in slightly different places on the sensor, and can be seen as colored fringing when images are examined closely. The D3200 has built-in correction for chromatic aberration during processing, but this applies only to JPEG images. Aberration can also be corrected in post-processing; with RAW images this is the only option.

Ideally, use lenses that minimize aberration in the first place. Although it's a

3

lens property, chromatic aberration can be exaggerated by the way light strikes a digital sensor. It's best to use lenses, such as Nikon's DX series, which are specifically designed for digital cameras.

Vignetting

Vignetting is a darkening towards the corners of the image. It's most conspicuous in even-toned areas like clear skies. Almost all lenses have a slight tendency to vignetting at maximum aperture, but it usually disappears on stopping down. Like most faults, it can be tackled in post-processing but prevention is better than cure.

Vignetting can also be caused, or exaggerated, by unsuitable lens hoods or filter holders, or by "stacking" multiple filters on the lens (rarely a good idea).

PERIOD SETTING ⌄
A vignette effect was added in post-processing. It enhances a "period" atmosphere, appropriate enough for this shot of an historic quayside. *32mm, 1/250 sec., f/10, ISO 200.*

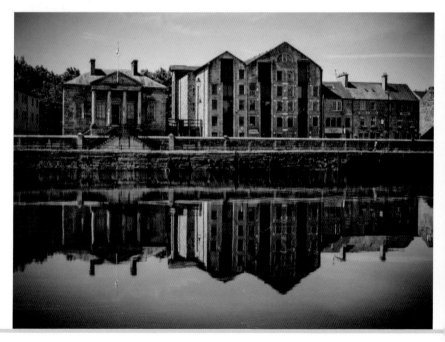

IMAGE PROPERTIES—DIGITAL

Noise

Image noise is created by random variations in the amount of light recorded by each pixel, and appears as speckles of varying brightness or color. It's most conspicuous in areas that should have an even tone, especially in the darker areas of the image. Unfortunately, noise becomes more prevalent as the individual photosites on the sensor get smaller, which results from cramming more megapixels onto the same size of sensor. However, this has driven big improvements in sensor technology and the associated software. Although the D3200 has more than 24 million photosites on its 23.2 x 15.4mm sensor, general noise levels are low, but noise does increase noticeably at the higher ISO settings.

To minimize noise, shoot at the lowest ISO rating possible and expose carefully: under-exposure increases the risk of visible noise. A tripod can be a big help. Noise reduction is often applied to JPEG images as part of in-camera processing but you may prefer to apply noise reduction to RAW files during postprocessing.

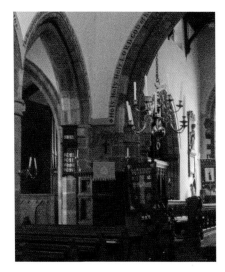

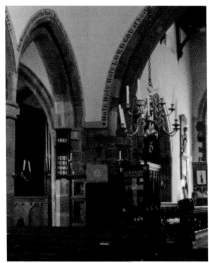

NOISES OFF »
This church interior was lit only by window light and the shot was taken at the maximum ISO setting. Noise is evident; the bottom image is after noise reduction was applied in Adobe Lightroom. *24mm, 1/50 sec., f/11, ISO 12,800.*

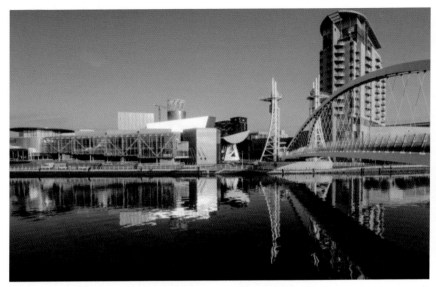

QUAY REFLECTION ⌃
At first glance, the exposure appears fine in this image, but all detail has been clipped or burned out in the highly reflective surface in the center of the image. *12mm, 1/60 sec., f/16, ISO 100.*

Clipping

Clipping occurs when either highlights or shadows are recorded without detail: i.e. shadows are a dead black and/or highlights are blank white. Clipping can be detected as a "spike" at either extreme of the histogram display, and in full-frame playback you can also opt to have the D3200 show highlight clipping by flashing affected areas of the image *(see page 93 under Display options).*

The D3200 is less prone to clipping than previous generations of cameras, but no camera is totally immune. There is some scope to recover clipped areas if you shoot RAW, while Active D-Lighting can help with JPEG images *(see page 86).*

Artefacts and aliasing

Normally when viewing a digital image we don't notice that it is made up of individual pixels, but small clumps of pixels can sometimes become apparent as "artefacts" of various kinds. They are usually more evident in low-resolution images, simply because of the smaller number (coarser "mapping") of pixels.

Aliasing is most evident on diagonal or curved lines, giving them a jagged or stepped appearance. Moiré or maze artefacts can occur when there's interference between areas of fine pattern in the subject and the grid pattern of the sensor itself. This often takes the form of aurora-like swirls or fringes of color. To compensate for such issues, digital cameras employ a low-pass filter directly in front of the sensor itself. This actually works by blurring the image slightly, and this is very effective in removing artefacts but means that images then need to be re-sharpened either in-camera or in post-processing (see below).

A further form of artefact is the JPEG artefact, which looks a lot like aliasing, but is created when JPEG images are compressed, either in-camera or on the computer. Avoid it by limiting JPEG compression: use the **Fine** setting for images that may later be printed or viewed at large sizes.

Sharpening images

Because of the low-pass filter, some sharpening is required to make digital camera images look acceptable. However, too much sharpening can produce artefacts, including white fringes or halos along defined edges.

JPEG images are sharpened during in-camera processing. Sharpening settings are accessed through the **Set Picture Control** item in the Shooting menu. Any changes to the sharpening level only affect images taken using that particular Picture

Tip

Repeatedly opening and re-saving JPEG images on the computer can multiply the effect of JPEG artefacts. If repeated edits are anticipated it's advisable to save the image as a TIFF first, and perform all editing operations on this version.

Control. It's nearly always wise to be conservative about in-camera sharpening levels. You can add more later, but it's virtually impossible to take it away again.

With RAW images, sharpening takes place on the computer, either during initial RAW conversion or later. Sharpening at the RAW conversion stage is reversible, because the original file is saved untouched; this means you can experiment with different levels of sharpening without permanent consequences.

A rare, perfectly still day—there was not a breath of wind even on the hilltops—meant that this cloud inversion lasted all day. Throughout the day I was looking for vantage points where I could set a solid foreground against the ethereal backdrop of misty, distant hills. This was about the best spot I found—though if I could have grown a bit taller and thereby "lowered" the foreground it might have given an even better sense of depth.

Settings
> Focal length: 125mm
> Shutter speed: 1/100 sec.
> Aperture: f/16
> Sensitivity: ISO 200
> Support: tripod

LAKE DISTRICT FELLS, UK

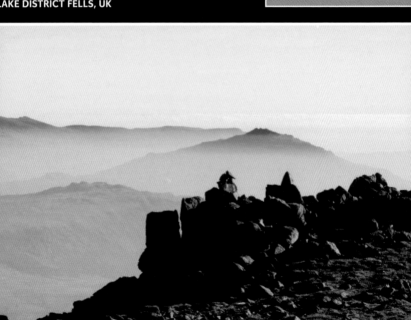

» GRAB SHOT

Candid photography or street photography—call it what you will—is part of a long and honorable tradition. You might suspect that Auto or Program mode would be logical choices for the quick-reaction "grab shot", but I chose Manual mode (and my second choice would have been Aperture-priority) as I wanted to set the lens to its widest aperture. This minimized depth of field, helping the subject stand out from a busy background, as well as keeping the shutter speed high.

Settings
> Focal length: 65mm
> Shutter speed: 1/640 sec.
> Sensitivity: ISO 200
> Aperture: f/2.8

ROYAL MILE, EDINBURGH, UK

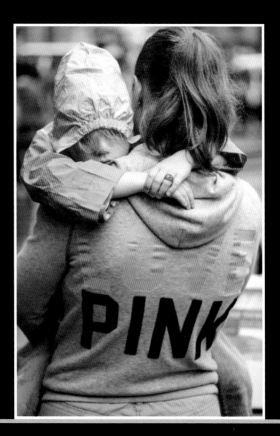

3 » MACRO

This was a mostly cloudy morning but, crucially, there was hardly any wind. At such close range (only just outside the minimum range of my 100mm macro lens) depth of field is minimal and the slightest movement, such as the flower swaying in the breeze, would have taken the insect completely out of focus. Because I couldn't keep myself 100% still either, I set the camera on a tripod to keep the distance constant. I focused manually as the fly's eye did not coincide with any of the D3200's 11 focus points.

Settings
> Focal length: 100mm macro
> Shutter speed: 1/250 sec.
> Aperture: f/11
> Sensitivity: ISO 200
> Support: tripod

NEAR GARSTANG, LANCASHIRE, UK

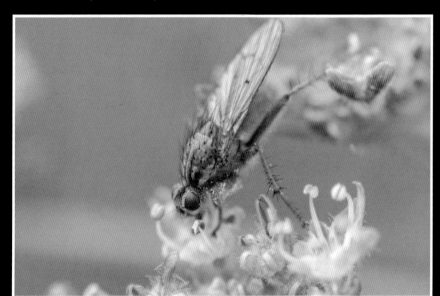

» ACTION AND PREFOCUSING

When shooting action, you can often identify promising spots before the event even starts. In a cyclo-cross event there will always be obstacles which require the riders to dismount and run for a short distance and I knew this would be a good place to stand for at least a couple of laps. As I was looking for action in the same place every time I didn't use autofocus but prefocused on the grass just in front of the

barrier. This left me free to concentrate on timing; with the rider's foot still in mid-air, and not too much clutter of other riders behind, this was one of the best shots from the day. A shutter speed of 1/640 sec. would not be fast enough for road-racing or even the faster sections in cyclo-cross, but was fast enough for the running sections.

Settings
> Focal length: 105mm
> Shutter speed: 1/640 sec.
> Aperture: f/9
> Sensitivity: ISO 800

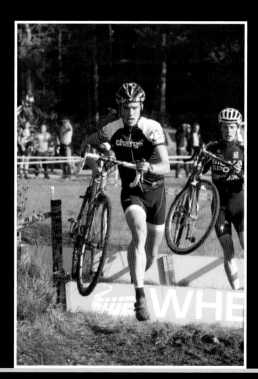

RAPHA SUPER CROSS SERIES

» "STUDIO" FLASH

I put "studio" in inverted commas because this tulip was actually set up on my dining room table. I draped a dark blanket over a chair to provide the black backdrop and lit the flower with two Speedlights, one from each side. I used Live View manual focus to make sure focus was exactly where I wanted it and took a couple of test shots to check the lighting balance. While I was using genuine Nikon Speedlights, there's absolutely no reason why this sort of result couldn't be replicated with the cheapest of flashguns—and if you use the "painting with light" approach *(see page 162)*, you only need one.

Settings
> Focal length: 50mm macro
> Shutter speed: 1/250 sec.
> Aperture: f/13
> Sensitivity: ISO 100
> Support: tripod

TULIP

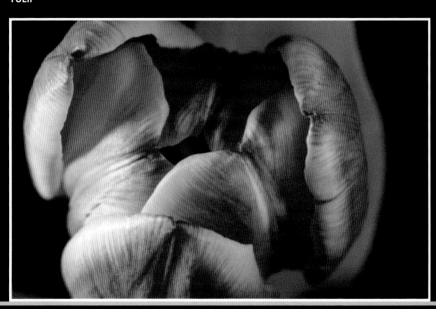

» "BAD" WEATHER

"There's no such thing as bad weather, only unsuitable clothing," said John Ruskin. You could equally say, "there's no such thing as bad weather, only inflexible photographers." Of course I was disappointed when we arrived on Barra and the sky wasn't blue, but the soft light was great for photographing flowers (there was a stunning display of orchids 50m from this beach). And it lent itself pretty well to moody landscape shots, emphasizing the gorgeous patterns and colors of the rocks in the foreground by getting low and close with a wide-angle lens. These rocks are Lewisian Gneiss—at 3 billion years old, among the oldest rocks in the world.

> **Settings**
> › Focal length: 18mm
> › Shutter speed: 1/30 sec.
> › Aperture: f/11
> › Sensitivity: ISO 100
> › Support: tripod

ISLE OF BARRA, WESTERN ISLES, UK

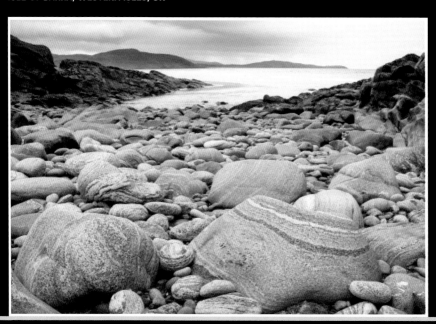

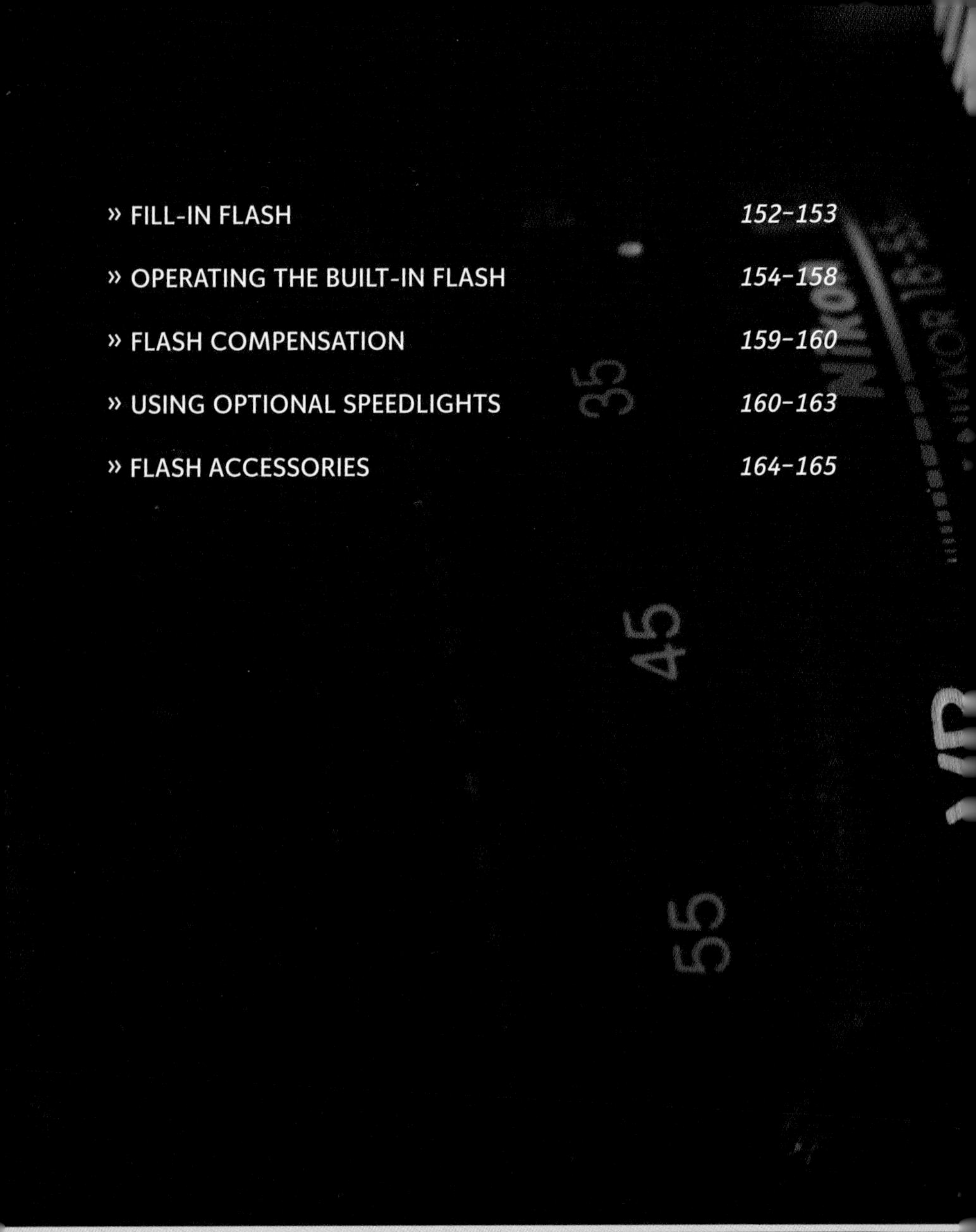
35
45
55

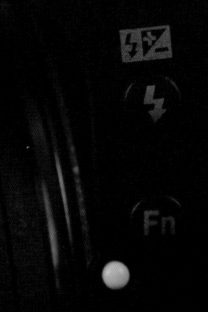

Chapter 4
FLASH

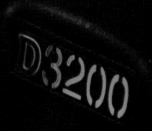

4 FLASH

Flash can be immensely useful to the photographer, but flash photography can also lead to great confusion and frustration if the fundamental principles are unclear. All flashguns are small. All flashguns are weak. These two statements are key to understanding flash photography. They are especially true for built-in units like that on the D3200 and most other DSLRs (those on compact cameras are typically even smaller and weaker).

Because it's small, the flash produces very hard light. It's similar to direct sunlight, but even the strongest sunlight is slightly softened by scattering and reflection; we can sometimes soften the flash, too.

The weakness of flash is even more fundamental. All flashguns have a limited range, and on-camera flash is more limited than most accessory flashguns.

Built-in flash units raise a third issue, too, namely their fixed position close to the lens, which makes the light one-dimensional—and the same for every shot, which is boring *(see Operating the built-in flash on page 154)*.

Flash is not the answer to every low-light shot. Understanding its limitations helps us understand when to seek alternatives, as well as when and how we can use flash effectively.

» FILL-IN FLASH

A key application for flash is for "fill-in" light, giving a lift to dark shadows like those cast by direct sunlight. This is why

Guide Numbers

The Guide Number (GN) is a measure of the power of a flash. In the past, photographers used GNs constantly to calculate flash exposures and working range. With modern flash metering, such computations are rarely needed, but the GN does help us compare different flashguns. For instance, the GN for the built-in flash is 12 (meters, ISO 100); for the Nikon SB-910 it is 34, indicating almost three times the power. This allows shooting at three times the distance, at a lower ISO, or with a smaller aperture.

Tip

GNs are specified in feet and/or metres and usually for an ISO rating of 100. When comparing different units, be sure that both GNs are stated in the same terms.

pros regularly use flash on bright days, exactly when most people would think it unnecessary.

Fill-in flash doesn't need to illuminate the shadows fully, only to lighten them a little. This means the flash can be used at a smaller aperture, or greater distance, than when it's the main light (averaging around two stops smaller, or four times the distance).

i-TTL balanced fill-flash for DSLR

Part of Nikon's Creative Lighting System (CLS), i-TTL balanced fill-flash helps achieve natural-looking results when using fill-in flash. It automatically applies provided (a) matrix or center-weighted metering is selected and (b) a CPU lens is attached.

The flash (built-in or compatible accessory flash) emits several virtually invisible pre-flashes immediately before exposure. Reflected light from these is analyzed by the metering sensor, together with the ambient light. If type D or G lenses are used, distance information is also incorporated.

Standard i-TTL flash for DSLR

When spot metering *(see page 49)* is selected, this mode is activated instead. Flash output is controlled to illuminate the subject correctly, but background illumination is not taken into consideration. This mode is appropriate when using flash as the main light source rather than for fill-in.

LIGHT ON THE SUBJECT ❯❯
The background exposure is the same for both shots, but without flash the foreground is virtually black. *22mm, 1/200 sec., f/11, ISO 200.*

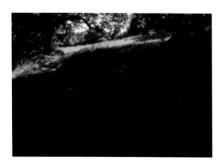
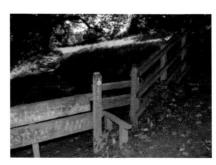

» OPERATING THE BUILT-IN FLASH

The built-in flash of the D3200, like all such units, is small, low-powered and fixed in position close to the lens axis. As well as limiting working range, these factors mean it produces a flat and harsh light which is unpleasant for, say, portraits. It may be better than nothing, but it only really comes into its own when used for fill-in light. The following assumes you are using P, S, A, or M modes; in Full Auto and Scene modes the flash activates either automatically or not at all.

To use the built-in flash

1) Select a metering method (see page 49): matrix or center-weighted metering is appropriate for fill-in flash using i-TTL balanced fill-flash. Spot metering is appropriate when flash is the main light.

2) Press ⚡. The flash pops up and begins charging. When it is charged, the ready indicator ⚡ is displayed in the viewfinder.

3) Choose a flash mode from the Active Information Display. Highlight the current flash mode (bottom left) and press **OK**. Select the desired flash mode and press **OK** again *(see pages 156–158).*

4) Half-press the shutter-release button to focus and take a meter reading. Fully depress the shutter-release button to take the photo.

5) When finished, lower the built-in flash by pressing down until it clicks into place.

Auto flash

In 🅰 Auto, 🏃 Portrait, 👶 Child, and 🌷 Close up modes, the default setting is **Auto flash**, which means that the flash will operate automatically if the camera judges that light levels are too low. Alternative modes which can be set are **Red-eye reduction** and **Flash off**. In 🌃 Night portrait mode the same basic modes apply, but Slow sync is possible *(see page 157).*

In 🅰 Auto (flash off), 🏔 Landscape, and 🏃 Sports modes, the effective mode is **Flash off** and this cannot be overridden (even if you fit a separate flashgun, the choices are limited to turning red-eye reduction on or off).

In P, S, A, or M modes, Auto flash is not available and you must activate the flash by pressing ⚡.

> ### Tip
>
> *The built-in flash is recommended for use with lenses between 18mm and 300mm focal length. Some lenses may block part of the flash output at close range; removing the lens hood often helps. The Nikon manual details limitations of use with certain lenses.*

Flash exposure

The combinations of shutter speed and aperture that are available when using flash depend on the exposure mode in use.

Exposure mode	Shutter speed	Aperture
AUTO Auto Portrait Child	Set automatically by the camera. The normal range is between 1/200 and 1/60 sec.	Set automatically by the camera.
P	Set automatically by the camera. The normal range is between 1/200 and 1/60 sec., but in certain flash modes all settings between 1/200 and 30 sec. are available.	Set automatically by the camera.
S Night portrait	Selected by user. All settings between 1/200 and 30 sec. are available. In S mode, if the user sets a faster shutter speed, the D3200 will fire at 1/200 sec. while the flash is active.	Set automatically by the camera.
A	Set automatically by the camera. The normal range is between 1/200 and 1/60 sec., but in certain flash modes all settings between 1/250 and 30 sec. are available.	Selected by user.
M	Selected by user. All settings between 1/200 and 30 sec. and bulb are available. If user sets a faster shutter speed, the D3200 will fire at 1/200 sec. when the flash is active.	Selected by user.

4

Flash range

The range of any flash depends on its power, ISO sensitivity setting and the aperture set. The table below details the approximate range of the built-in flash for selected distances, apertures and ISO settings. These figures are based on the table in the D3200 manual, confirmed by practical tests; there's no need to memorize them, but it helps to understand the limited range that applies when using flash. A quick test shot will show if a subject is within range in any given situation.

Tip

If flash appears too weak, or the range is insufficient, turning up the ISO setting may help, but check first that flash compensation (see page 159) is not in effect.

› Flash synchronization and flash modes

Flash, as the name implies, is virtually instantaneous. A burst of flash lasts just a few milliseconds. In order to cover the whole image frame, the flash must be fired when the shutter is fully open. However, at faster shutter speeds SLRs like the D3200 do not in fact expose the whole frame at once. In the case of the D3200, the fastest shutter speed which can be used with flash is 1/200 sec. This is known as the sync (for synchronization) speed.

The D3200 has several flash modes—the differences between them are largely to do with synchronization and shutter speed. Choose a flash mode by pressing ⚡ and rotating the Command Dial. (In P, S, A, or M modes press the button once to raise the flash, then press again and rotate the Command Dial to choose flash mode.)

	ISO setting					Range	
	100	200	400	800	1600	meters	feet
	1.4	2	2.8	4	5.6	1.0–8.5	3' 3"–27'
	2	2.8	4	5.6	8	0.7–6.1	2' 4"–20'
	2.8	4	5.6	8	11	0.6–4.2	2'–13'.9"
	4	5.6	8	11	16	0.6–3.0	2'–9' 10"
Aperture	5.6	8	11	16	22	0.6–2.1	2'–6' 11"
	8	11	16	22	32	0.6–1.5	2'–4' 11"
	11	16	22	32		0.6–1.1	2'–3' 7"
	16	22	32			0.6–0.8	2'–2' 7"

Flash mode can also be selected through the Active Information Display—the flash item appears bottom left—or the Guide menu (under Advanced operation).

Auto flash mode

This is the default flash mode when using P, S, A, or M exposure modes, and is ideal for fast response. In standard flash operation, the flash fires as soon as the shutter is fully open, i.e. as soon as possible after the shutter-release button is pressed. In P and A exposure modes, the camera will set a shutter speed in the range 1/60–1/200 sec.

Slow sync (front-curtain sync)

This mode allows longer shutter speeds (up to 30 seconds) to be used in P, A and 🌃 Night portrait exposure modes, so that backgrounds can be captured even in low ambient light. Movement of the subject or

camera (or even both) can result in a partly blurred image combined with a sharp image where the subject is lit by the flash. This may be unwanted, but can also be used intentionally for creative effect.

This mode is also available, in a limited form (longest exposure of 1 second), with 🌃 Night portrait mode. You can't select slow sync in S and M exposure modes, but it isn't necessary, as longer shutter speeds are available anyway (i.e. standard flash mode and slow sync mode are effectively the same).

In this mode, the flash fires as soon as the shutter is fully open, which is why it's called front-curtain sync. It can create odd-looking results when dealing with moving subjects. The "opposite" of front-curtain sync is, naturally enough, rear-curtain sync—see below.

Rear-curtain sync

Rear-curtain sync triggers the flash not at the first available moment (as per front-curtain sync) but at the last possible instant. This makes sense when photographing moving subjects because any image of the subject created by the ambient light then appears behind the sharp flash image, which looks more

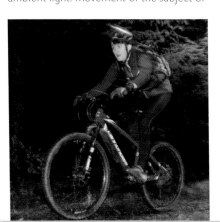

Front-curtain sync in action «
Slow sync combines a flash image with a motion-blurred image from the ambient light, but front-curtain sync makes the movement trail ahead of the flash image, not behind it.

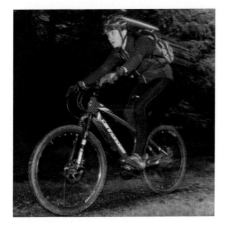

Rear-curtain sync in action
Rear-curtain sync means that the motion-blurred part of the image trails behind the sharp image created by the flash.

natural than having it appear to extend ahead of the direction of movement. Rear-curtain sync can only be selected when using P, S, A, or M exposure modes. In P and A modes it also allows slow shutter speeds (below 1/60 sec.) to be used, and is then called **slow rear curtain sync**.

When using longer exposure times, shooting with rear-curtain sync can be tricky, as you need to predict where your subject will be at the end of the exposure, rather than immediately after pressing the shutter-release button. It is often best suited to working with cooperative subjects or naturally repeating action, so that you can fine-tune the timing after reviewing images on the monitor.

Red-eye reduction

On-camera flash, especially from built-in units, is very prone to "red-eye", where light reflects off the subject's retina. Red-eye reduction works by shining a light on the subject about a second before the exposure, causing their pupils to contract. This delay makes it inappropriate with moving subjects, and kills spontaneity. It's generally better to remove red-eye using the Red-eye correction facility in the Retouch menu *(see page 108)* or on the computer. Better still, use a separate flash, well away from the lens axis, or no flash at all, perhaps shooting at a high ISO rating.

Red-eye reduction with slow sync

This combines the two modes named, allowing backgrounds to register. This mode is only available when using P and A exposure modes and ⛰ Night portrait.

FLASH COMPENSATION

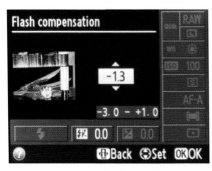

Flash compensation in the Active Information Display

Tip

Flash compensation can also be set by pressing ⚡ *and* 🗲 *and rotating the Command Dial. As the figures are displayed on the screen anyway, it seems easier to use the Active Information Display.*

Although the D3200's flash metering is extremely sophisticated, you may still want to adjust flash output, perhaps for creative effect. Playing back images on the monitor makes it easy to assess the effect of the flash level, allowing compensation to be applied with confidence to further shots. To use flash compensation, activate the Active Information Display. The flash compensation item is midway along the

bottom of the screen. Compensation can be set from −3 Ev to +1 Ev in increments of ⅓ Ev. Positive compensation will brighten areas lit by the flash, while leaving other

BEAR LIGHTING ☒
The three shots were taken with flash compensation set to +1, 0 and −1 respectively. The flash has no effect on the background—which is in daylight—because it's effectively out of range. *86mm, 1/30 sec., f/5.6, ISO 400.*

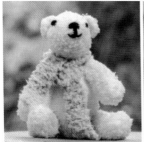
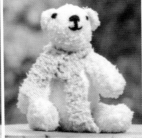
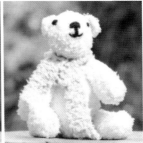

areas of the image unaffected. However, if the flash is already at the limit of its range, positive compensation can't make it any brighter.

Negative compensation reduces the brightness of flash-lit areas, again leaving other areas unaffected. After use, reset the flash compensation level to zero. Otherwise the camera will retain the setting next time flash is used. Flash compensation works similarly when a compatible Speedlight like the SB-910 or SB-700 is attached.

Manual flash

If **Flash cntrl for built-in flash** in the Shooting menu is set to **Manual**, you can control flash output even more precisely, from full power to as low as ⅟₃₂ power.

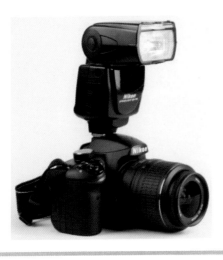

» USING OPTIONAL SPEEDLIGHTS

If you're serious about portrait or close-up photography, in particular, you'll soon find the built-in flash inadequate. Accessory flashguns, which Nikon calls Speedlights, enormously extend the power and flexibility of flash with the D3200.

Nikon Speedlights integrate fully with Nikon's Creative Lighting System for outstanding results using flash. There are currently four models, all highly sophisticated units mainly aimed at professional and advanced users, and priced accordingly. The flagship SB-910 is particularly impressive—but at a price approaching that of a D3200 body!

Independent makers such as Sigma offer alternatives, some of them also compatible with Nikon's i-TTL flash control. However such "dedicated" units are also hardly cheap.

Many possibilities can be explored with much cheaper units. For instance, any flashgun, however basic, that allows manual triggering with a "test" button can be used for the "painting with light" technique outlined below. You may have an old flashgun at the back of a cupboard, and it's also worth checking the bargain bin at the local camera shop.

FLASHGUN   «
D3200 with a Nikon SB-700 Speedlight.

› Mounting an external Speedlight

1) Check that the camera and the Speedlight are both switched off, and that the pop-up flash is down. Remove the hotshoe cover.

2) Slide the foot of the Speedlight into the camera's hotshoe. If it does not slide easily, check whether the mounting lock on the Speedlight is in the locked position.

3) Rotate the lock lever at the base of the Speedlight to secure it in position.

4) Switch on both the camera and the Speedlight.

› Bounce flash and off-camera flash

The fixed position of the built-in flash throws shadows on close subjects and gives portraits a "police mugshot" look. A separate Speedlight mounted in the hotshoe improves things slightly, but you can make a much bigger difference by either:

1) Bouncing the flash light off a ceiling, wall or reflector.

2) Taking the Speedlight off the camera.

Tip

Speedlights are greedy for battery power and it is always wise to carry at least one set of spares.

› Bounce flash

Bouncing the flash light off a suitable surface both spreads the light, softening hard-edged shadows, and changes its direction, producing better modeling on the subject.

Nikon's SB-910 and SB-700 Speedlights have heads which can be tilted and swiveled through a wide range, allowing light to be bounced off walls, ceilings and other surfaces. The SB-400 has a more limited tilt capability, allowing light to be bounced off the ceiling or a reflector.

Tip

Most surfaces will absorb some of the light, and in any case the light has to travel further to reach the subject; i-TTL metering will automatically adjust for this, but the effective range is reduced. However, many accessory flashguns do have more power than the built-in unit.

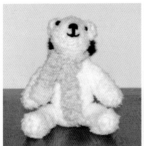 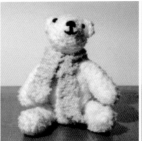 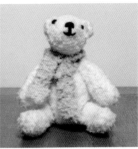

› Off-camera flash

Taking the flash off the camera gives you complete control over the direction of its light. The flash can be fired using a remote cord; Nikon's dedicated cords preserve i-TTL metering *(see Chapter 8, page 221)*.

› Painting with light

You can try this technique with any flashgun that can be triggered manually. By firing multiple flashes at the subject from different directions, you build up overall coverage of light without losing the sparkle that directional light gives.

1) Set up so that neither camera nor subject can move during the exposure.

2) Use Manual mode. Set a long shutter speed such as 20 or 30 sec., or even B. Set a small aperture such as f/16 (this may need trial and error). Focus on the subject then turn the focus selector to M so the camera doesn't try to refocus.

BEAR SHADOWS ⌃
The first shot was taken using the built-in flash; there are a couple of ugly shadows, but otherwise everything looks flat. The second uses indirect flash from the left, giving much more interesting light and depth. The third image uses bounce flash to give a much softer, more even light, without losing the 3D quality. *55mm, 1/200 sec., f/11, ISO 100.*

FRUIT FLASH ⌄
This shot used four bursts of flash, one each from left front, left rear, right front and right rear. *50mm, 10 sec., f/16, ISO 400.*

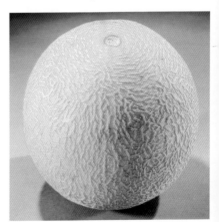

3) Turn out the lights. It helps to have just enough background light to see what you are doing, but no more.

4) Trip the shutter and then fire the flash at the subject from different directions (without aiming directly into the lens).

5) Review the result and start again! For example, if results are too bright, use fewer flashes, a lower ISO, a smaller aperture, fire from further away, or a combination. If the flash has a variable power setting this could be turned down.

› Nikon Speedlights

The table summarizes key features of current Nikon Speedlights.

› Wireless flash

Nikon's Creative Lighting System includes the ability to regulate the light from multiple Speedlights through a wireless system. The SB-910 and SB-700 Speedlights can be used as the "commander" unit for a wireless setup. There's also a stand-alone commander unit, the SU-800.

The Speedlight SB-R200 works only as part of such a system, not as a stand-alone flash. Nikon uses this unit in its close-up flash system (see the Close-up chapter for more detail, page 166).

	SB-910	SB-700	SB-400	SB-R200
Flash coverage (lens focal length range)	12–200	14–120	18–27	24
Guide number (ISO 100 meters}	34	28	21	10
Twist/swivel	Yes	Yes	Tilt only	No
Dimensions (width x height x depth - mm)	78.5 x 145 x 113	71 x 126 x 104.5	66 x 56.5 x 80	80 x 75 x 55
Weight (without batteries)	420g	360g	127g	120g
Use as Commander	Yes	Yes	No	No*

* Cannot be used in camera hotshoe, only as a slave within Creative Lighting System

» FLASH ACCESSORIES

To add even more flexibility and control of lighting effects, a wide variety of flash accessories is available. Nikon has an extensive range, but when time is short or money is tight substitutes for some of these can be improvized.

› Battery packs

Nikon produces add-on power packs for some of its Speedlights to speed up recycling and extend battery life.

› Color filters

Flash filters can be used to create striking color effects, or to match the color of the flash to that of the background lighting. Nikon produces various filters to fit its Speedlight range.

› Flash cords

Because the D3200's built-in flash can't act as a wireless commander, you can only maintain full metering and control of an external Speedlight if it's physically connected to the camera, either in the hotshoe or using a flash cord (also known as a sync lead). Dedicated cords like Nikon's SC-28 allow full communication between camera and Speedlight, retaining i-TTL flash control. The SC-28 extends up to 5ft (1.5m).

› Flash diffusers

Flash diffusers are a simple, economical way to spread and soften the hard light from a flashgun. They may slide over the flash head or be attached by low-tech means like elastic bands or Velcro. Sto-Fen make Omni-Bounce diffusers to fit most flashguns, and an Omni-Flip for built-in units like the D3200's. Even a white handkerchief can be used at a pinch.

GET CONNECTED ⌄
Connecting a flashgun using a flash cord.

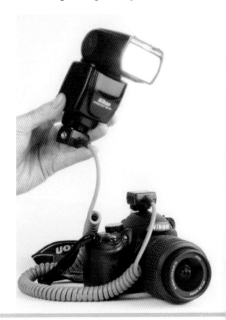

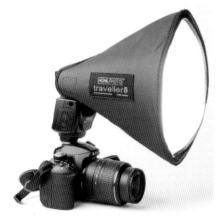

READY DIFFUSION ⌃
A D3200 and flashgun with a HONL "softbox".

Diffusers reduce the light reaching the subject; the D3200's metering system will allow for this, but the effective range will be shorter.

A step beyond a simple diffuser is the portable "softbox" which can attach to a Speedlight to create a wider spread of light.

› Flash extenders

A flash extender slips over the flash head, using mirrors or a lens to create a tighter beam and extend the effective range of the flash. Again, the D3200's metering system will automatically accommodate the use of an extender. Nikon do not make flash-extenders, so a third-party option will be required.

› Flash brackets

The ability to mount the flash off-camera, and therefore change the angle at which the light hits the subject, is invaluable in controlling the quality of light. Nikon's Speedlights can be mounted on a tripod or stand on any flat surface using the AS-19 stand, but for a more portable solution many photographers prefer a light, flexible arm or bracket which attaches to the camera and supports the Speedlight. Novoflex produces a range of such products.

MELON BALL ⌄
An alternative take to the shot on page 162. Taken with a time-honored set-up: one flashgun off to the right and a second, at half-power, on the left. *50mm, f/11, ISO 400.*

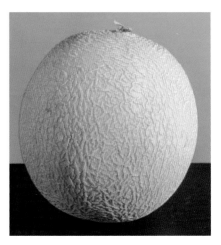

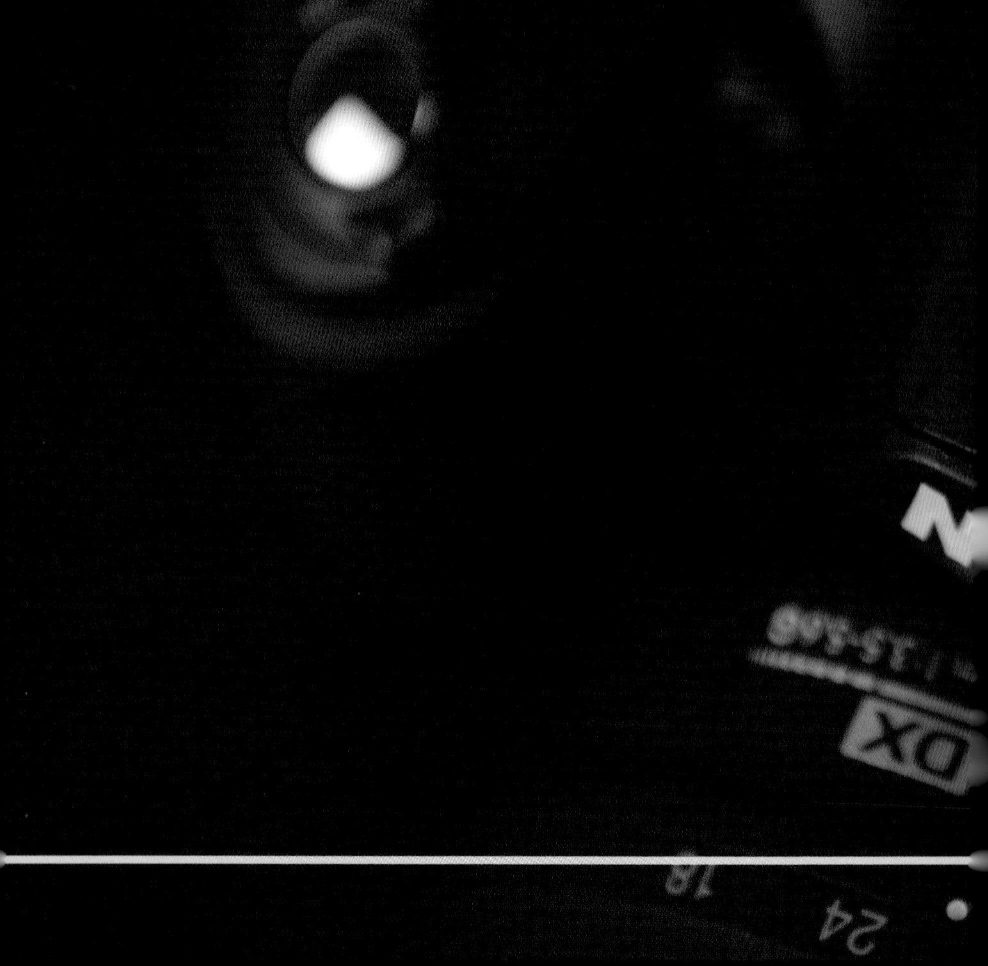

Chapter 5
CLOSE-UP

5 CLOSE-UP

Most photography is about capturing what you can see with the naked eye. Close-up photography goes beyond this into a whole new world, or at least a new way of seeing the world. For close-up photography the 35mm film SLR and its digital successors like the Nikon D3200 reign supreme. Reflex viewing, once essential in close-up work, is now supplemented by Live View. Also, the D3200 is part of the legendary Nikon system of lenses and other accessories, which offers many additional options for close-up photography.

Depth of field *(see page 119)* is a key issue. As you move closer to the subject, depth of field becomes narrower. This has several consequences. First, it's often necessary to stop down to small apertures, which can make long exposures essential. Second, the slightest movement of either subject or camera can ruin the focus. For both reasons, a tripod or other solid camera support is often required. It may also be necessary to prevent the subject from moving (within ethical limits, of course!)

Because depth of field is so slim, focusing becomes critical. Merely focusing

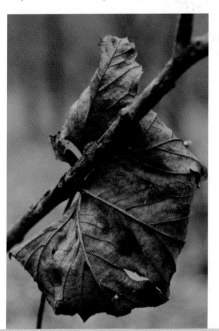

Tip

To get as close as possible to the subject, use manual focus and set the lens at minimum focusing distance. Don't touch the focus control again. Instead move either camera or subject until the image is sharp. Though slow, this guarantees you're as close as the lens will allow.

OLD LEAF «
Close-up subjects are everywhere, and close-up photography really opens our eyes to them. *70mm, 1/125 sec., f/5.6, ISO 800.*

on "the subject" is no longer adequate and you may have to decide which part of the subject—an insect's eye, the stamen of a flower—should be the point of sharp focus. With its 11 AF points, the D3200 can focus accurately within much of the frame, but this is also where Live View mode comes into its own. By selecting 〖 〗 Wide-area AF or 〖 〗 Normal area AF *(see page 74)*, the focus point can be set anywhere in the frame. If you prefer to use manual focus, Live View—with its zoomable view—also makes this ultra-precise.

Macro photography

There's no exact definition of "close-up," but "macro" should be used more precisely. Macro photography really means photography of objects at life-size or larger, implying a reproduction ratio (see below) of at least 1:1. Many zoom lenses are branded "macro" when their reproduction ratio is around 1:4, or 1:2 at best. This still allows much fascinating close-up photography, but it isn't "proper" macro.

Reproduction ratio

The reproduction ratio is the ratio between the actual size of the subject and the size of its image on the D3200's imaging sensor, which measures 23.2 x 15.4mm. At 1:1 an object of these dimensions would exactly fill the image frame. SD memory cards are close to this size. When the image is printed, or displayed on a computer

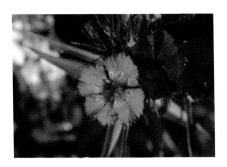

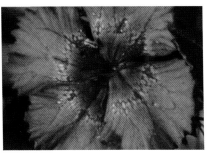

ZOOM WITH A VIEW ⌃
The first shot shows the closest view with a "normal" 18–55mm zoom lens (approximately 1:3). The second, taken with a 50mm macro lens at the closest possible distance, gives approximately life size (1:1) reproduction. *55mm and 50mm macro, 1/400 sec. at f/11 and 1/200 sec. at f/11, ISO 200, both ISO 200.*

screen, it may appear many times larger, but that's another story.

A 1:4 reproduction ratio means that the smallest subject that would give you a frame-filling shot is one that's four times as long/wide as the sensor. With the D3200 this is roughly 4 x 2½ inches (or 94 x 63mm)—slightly larger than a credit card.

for 1:1 reproduction is double that of a 100mm. Because the D3200's sensor is smaller than a 35mm film frame, the effective focal length of any lens is multiplied by approx 1.5x, and therefore working distance increases also. This is often helpful with living subjects which are susceptible to disturbance.

Working distance

The working distance is the distance required to obtain the desired reproduction ratio with any given lens. It is related to the focal length of the lens: with a 200mm macro lens the working distance

CLOSE BUD ⌄

This demonstrates the minimal depth of field obtained in extreme close-up work, at about 1:3 reproduction ratio. Careful focusing ensures the sharp zone is exactly where it's wanted. *50mm macro, 1/640 sec., f/5.6, ISO 400.*

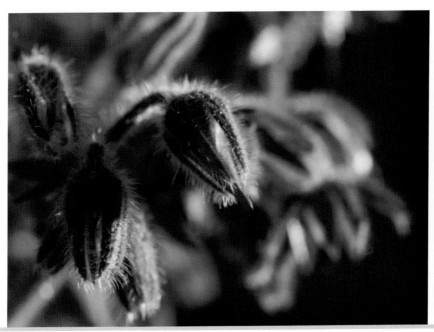

EQUIPMENT FOR CLOSE-UP PHOTOGRAPHY

› Close-up attachment lenses

These simple magnifying lenses screw into the filter thread of the lens. They are light, portable, (relatively) inexpensive and fully compatible with the camera's exposure and focusing systems.

Nikon produces seven close-up attachment lenses *(see table below)*.

› Extension tubes

Extension tubes are another simple, relatively inexpensive, way of extending the close-focusing capabilities of a lens. An extension tube is essentially a simple tube fitting between the lens and the camera. This decreases the minimum focusing distance and thereby increases the magnification factor. Again they are light, compact and easy to carry and attach.

The Nikon system includes four Extension tubes, PK-11A, PK-12, PK-13, and PN-11, which extend the lens by 8mm, 14mm, 27.5mm, and 52.5mm respectively. The PK-11 incorporates a tripod mount. The basic design of these tubes has not changed for many years, which means that many of the camera's functions are not available. In particular, there's no autofocus. On the D3200 these tubes must be used in Manual (M) mode and exposure determination is by trial and error—but that's what playback and the histogram are for! If you're prepared to use the D3200 in a good old-fashioned way, they are almost certainly the best low-cost way into true macro photography.

> **Tip**
>
> *Compatible extension tubes are also produced by other manufacturers, notably Kenko. These do support exposure metering but still do not permit autofocus on the D3200.*

Product number	Attaches to filter thread	Recommended for use with
0, 1, 2	52mm	Standard lenses
3T, 4T	52mm	Short telephoto lenses
5T, 6T	62mm	Telephoto lenses

5

› Bellows

Bellows work on the same principle as extension tubes, by extending the spacing between the lens and the camera body, but are not restricted to a few set lengths.

> *Note:*
> Because accessories like extension tubes and bellows increase the effective physical length of the lens, they also increase the effective focal length. However, the physical size of the aperture does not change. The result is to make the lens "slower"; that is, a lens with a maximum aperture of f/2.8 starts to behave like an f/4 or f/5.6 lens. This makes the viewfinder image dimmer than normal, and affects the exposure required. Reversing rings do not have this effect.

Again, there's no extra glass to impair the optical quality of the lens. However, bellows are expensive, heavy and cumbersome, and take time to set up. They are usually employed in controlled settings, such as a studio.

Nikon's PB-6 bellows offer extensions from 48mm to 208mm, giving a maximum reproduction ratio of about 11:1. Focusing and exposure are manual only.

› Reversing rings

Also known as reverse adapters, or—in Nikon's jargon—inversion rings, these allow lenses to be mounted in reverse; the adapter screws into the filter thread. This allows much closer focusing than when the lens is used normally. Ideally used with a prime lens, a reversing ring could be coupled with an inexpensive old manual focus 50mm f/1.8. Nikon's inversion ring BR-2A fits a 52mm filter thread.

MACRO LENSES

True macro lenses achieve reproduction ratios of 1:1 or better and are optically optimized for close-up work, though normally very capable for general photography too. This is certainly true of Nikon's Micro Nikkor lenses, of which there are currently five.

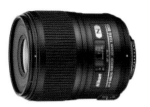

60mm f/2.8G ED AF-S Micro Nikkor

The most recent addition to the range is the 40mm f/2.8G AF-S DX Micro Nikkor; like the 85mm model (see below) it's specifically designed for DX format cameras like the D3200. It's also Nikon's least expensive macro lens.

The 60mm f/2.8G ED AF-S Micro Nikkor is an upgrade to the previous 60mm f/2.8D: advances include ED glass for superior optical quality and Silent Wave Motor for ultra-quiet autofocus.

The 85mm f/3.5G ED VR AF-S DX Micro Nikkor also achieves 1:1 reproduction and has VRII, internal focusing and ED glass.

The 105mm f/2.8G AF-S VR Micro Nikkor also features internal focusing, ED glass and Silent Wave Motor—it was also the world's first macro lens with VR (Vibration Reduction). As the slightest camera shake is magnified at high reproduction ratios, technology designed to combat its effects is extremely welcome,

allowing you to employ shutter speeds up to four stops slower than otherwise possible. However, though it may neutralize camera shake, it has no effect on subject movement.

Though rather more venerable, the 200mm f/4D ED-IF AF Micro Nikkor is particularly favored for shooting the animal kingdom, as its longer working distance reduces the risk of disturbing your subject. This lens lacks a built-in motor and so can't autofocus with the D3200—this might be an issue with animal work but is easily accommodated for static subjects.

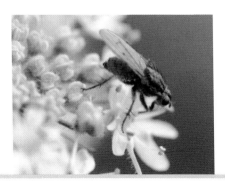

ON THE FLY 》
Longer lenses are very useful for some subjects—especially highly mobile ones! *100mm macro, 1/200 sec., f/11, ISO 200, tripod.*

5 » MACRO LIGHTING

We've already observed that macro photography often requires small apertures. This may lead to long exposure times, creating particular problems with mobile subjects. Additional lighting is often required, which usually means flash. However, regular Speedlights are not designed for close-range use. If mounted on the hotshoe, the short working distance means that the lens may throw a shadow on the subject. The built-in flash is even less suitable for real close-up work, yet in 🌷 Close-up mode it regularly pops up automatically; perhaps it should be called "Not too close" mode instead.

Specialist macro flash units usually take the form of either ring-flash or twin flash.

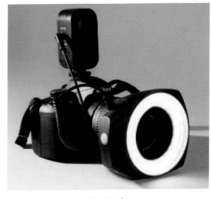

Sunpak LED Macro Ring Light

PETAL POWER

This shot was taken with the Sunpak Ring Light. Simple lighting often suits complex subjects. *50mm macro, 0.6 sec., f/11, ISO 400, tripod.*

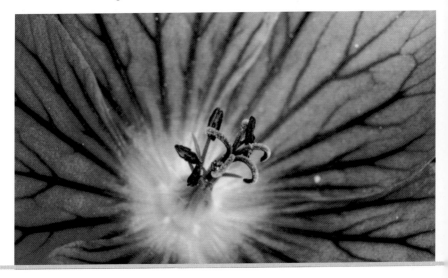

Because of the close operating distances they do not need high power and can be relatively light and compact.

Ring-flash units encircle the lens, giving an even spread of light even on ultra-close subjects (they're also favored by some portrait photographers). Nikon's discontinued SB-29s may still be found at some dealers, while alternatives come from Sigma and Marumi.

Nikon now concentrates on a twin-flash approach with its Speedlight Commander Kit R1C1 and Speedlight Remote Kit R1. These are both based around two Speedlight SB-R200 flashguns which mount either side of the lens. The R1C1 uses a Wireless Speedlight Commander SU-800 unit which fits into the camera's hot shoe, while the R1 requires a separate Speedlight as commander. These kits are expensive but they do give very flexible and precisely controllable light on macro subjects.

An alternative is to use LED lights, like the Sunpak LED Macro Ring Light. Its continuous output allows you to preview the image in a way not possible with flash. However, its low power limits it to close, and usually static, subjects. But then again, it is very cheap!

› Improvization

Dedicated macro flash units aren't cheap, and may be unaffordable or unjustifiable when you just want a taste of macro work. Fortunately, you can do lots with a standard flashgun, plus a flash cord. With more basic units, you'll lose the D3200's advanced flash control, but it only takes a few test shots to establish settings that you can use repeatedly (remember to keep notes!). The other essential is a small reflector, perhaps just a piece of white card. Position it as close as possible to the subject for maximum benefit.

This set-up (used for several example shots in this book) can even be more flexible than twin flash or ring-flash, allowing the light to be directed wherever you choose. On static subjects, "painting with light" *(see page 162)* is also an interesting option.

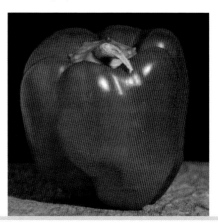

SIMPLY RED »
This shot was taken with the simplest of set-ups: a flashgun at around 45 degrees on the right and a white card reflector just out of frame on the left.
150mm macro, 1/125 sec., f/10, ISO 100.

Chapter 6
MOVIES

6 MOVIES

The ability to record moving images is now widespread among DSLRs, but it was as recently as August 2008 that the Nikon D90 became the first DSLR from any manufacturer to offer this feature. The movie mode is really an extension of Live View *(see page 71)*, and therefore familiarity with Live View is a big asset when you start shooting movies.

› Movie size and quality

The D3200 can shoot movies in Full HD (high definition) quality with a frame size of 1920 x 1080 pixels. You can plug the camera into an HD TV and play your movie clips right off. However, a collection of clips is not a movie *(see Editing on page 190)*. After editing, getting your movies on to your TV

is not quite so simple, and usually requires a DVD or Blu-Ray writer and player.

You can upload Full HD movies to YouTube's HD channel, but only viewers with a really fast internet connection will be able to view it without stuttering. There's one other obvious destination for Full HD movies—the latest iPad.

Most other mobile devices, and most current Mac and PC monitors have lower resolution. The D3200 also allows you to select frame sizes of 1280 x 720 (or "720p")

RIVER WIDE ⌄
The D3200 allows wide-angle shooting; a 14mm lens was used here.

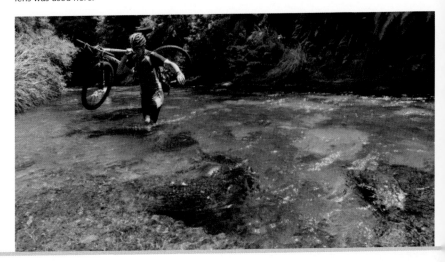

and 640 x 424 pixels. 720p is the standard on Vimeo, the real home of quality video online, and will look excellent on most computer screens. The smallest size is fine for standard YouTube video and the majority of mobile devices.

These lower settings allow you to record more video on the same memory card, as well as consuming less disk space on your computer. A 4Gb card will hold a little over 20 minutes of footage at the highest quality setting, almost 2 hours at the lowest.

The D3200 produces movies in a standard Motion-JPEG format (the file extension is .AVI) which can be played through standard media players such as QuickTime, RealPlayer and Windows Media Player.

To choose size and quality settings, *see page 183.*

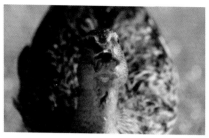

SHALLOW SHOT ⌃
It's much easier to get really shallow depth of field than with most video cameras—especially when using longer lenses (this is a 300mm).

achieve very shallow depth of field, which is virtually unattainable with compact cameras or camcorders. This can give some very striking effects, and is one of the strongest features of the D3200's movie mode.

The D3200's large sensor and high-ISO shooting ability mean that results in low light should be better than most of the

› Advantages

Today many compact cameras and camcorders also deliver HD resolution, but because the D3200 has a larger sensor, its image quality is superior in many respects. It can also use the entire array of Nikon-fit lenses *(see chapter 7, page 194),* giving a range that is difficult to match with any conventional video camera, especially for wide-angle shooting.

Another plus is that the D3200's larger sensor and ability to use lenses with wide maximum apertures mean it's possible to

Note:
Most digital video cameras claim enormous zoom ranges (often 800x or more) but these are only achieved by "digital zoom", which is a software function that enlarges the central portion of the image. Anything more than a small amount of digital zoom results in an obvious loss of image quality. "Optical zoom" range is what really matters, and the D3200's interchangeable lenses give a potential range of at least 50x (12mm–600mm). The widest range currently available in a single lens is 18–300mm.

6

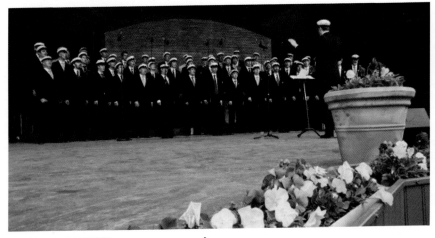

SINGING IN THE DARK ⌃
The D3200 also scores when it comes to low-light shooting.

alternatives. In addition, the full range of exposure modes, Nikon Picture Controls and many other options can be used, giving a high level of creative control. (In practice, however, P, S, A and M modes are less flexible when shooting movies than when shooting stills.)

› Limitations

Functionally, the D3200's movie mode is among the best of any current DSLR, but some limitations remain. The viewing system makes handheld shooting awkward (the D5100, with its fold-out screen, has an edge here) and Live View AF isn't slick enough for fast-moving subjects. Sound quality from the built-in microphone is

at best moderate (though you can attach a separate microphone). One other limitation: you cannot record a clip longer than 20 minutes. However, for the viewer of your movies this is a good thing!

› Image effects

The D3200, like other DSLRs, captures video by a "rolling" scan, rather than capturing the whole frame at one go. This has an odd effect when dealing with fast movement, whether it's a rapid pan of the camera or movement of the subject itself: objects appear distorted, with rectangular shapes turning to parallelograms and so on. Rocking the camera from side to side can achieve a wobbly effect known as "jello-cam". Some movie-editing software can now compensate.

» MAKING MOVIES

› Focus options

The D3200 uses the same focusing options as Live View *(see page 72)*, including manual focus. If you're familiar with Live View AF, you'll be aware of its limitations when faced with fast-moving subjects, and this is something that must be factored in when planning a movie shot.

While the quality of the Live View display does make manual focusing fairly easy, at least in good light, it is hard to operate the controls really smoothly, especially when handholding the camera *(see Shooting, on page 185)*.

› Focusing

The D3200 will automatically maintain focus while movie recording is in progress, provided Full-time servo AF (AF-F) is selected first, though it may lag behind rapid camera movements. If Single-servo AF (AF-S) is selected the camera will only refocus when you half-press the shutter-release button, and this is often all too obvious in the final movie clip. However, keeping half-pressure on the button is one way of locking focus.

Manual focusing is also possible, but can be yet another recipe for wobbly pictures. Yet again, the use of a tripod is recommended, especially with longer

Warning!

Older lenses (any lens lacking a CPU) can only be used on the D3200 in M manual mode, and exposure setting is by trial and error. This can be done fairly quickly by shooting a few still frames and checking the histogram *(see page 84)*. Some such lenses may still be worth using because of their smooth focusing movement.

lenses, where focusing is more critical and wobbles are magnified. Some lenses may have a smoother manual focus action, and the physical design of older lenses often makes them more suitable, with large and well placed focus rings. Older lenses often have a distance scale marked on the lens barrel, which can offer a viable alternative to using the Live View display to focus. Pre-focusing manually also avoids undesirable focus shifts during shooting.

Using a fixed focus for each shot is often perfectly viable, especially when depth of field is good. This reduces operations which can make the shot wobbly and avoids distracting shifts of focus in mid-shot.

Study the credits for major movies and TV shows and you'll often see someone called a "focus puller". This is an assistant to the camera operator, whose sole task is to adjust the focus, normally between predetermined points (for instance, shifting from one character's face to another). This leaves the lead camera operator free to concentrate on framing, panning and zooming. Frequently, the focus puller uses the distance scale on the lens barrel, relying on previously measured distances. While this may seem a far cry from shooting simple movie clips on the D3200, it does suggest that it could be worth trying a bit of teamwork, especially if you want to pan or zoom at the same time as adjusting focus.

› Exposure

Exposure control depends on the exposure mode selected before shooting begins. If Auto or Scene modes are selected, exposure control is fully automatic, except that in Scene modes exposure level can be locked using the **AE-L/AF-L** button. This is useful, for instance, to avoid annoying changes in brightness as you pan across a scene.

If P, S, A, or M mode is selected, exposure levels can be adjusted by ±3 Ev using 🔳 and the Command Dial—just like exposure compensation *(see page 50)* in stills shooting.

In A mode, the Command Dial can be rotated during shooting and the aperture setting in the on-screen display will change accordingly, but the actual aperture in use does not change until the

clip ends and you start shooting a new clip. The readouts may also show impossible shutter speeds. This creates an illusion of manual control. The only way to adjust exposure in mid-shot is with 🔳 and the Command Dial together.

In M mode, you can set shutter speed and ISO directly, provided you've enabled Manual movie settings (see below). You can (if the light's good) set shutter speeds right up to 1/4000 sec., but there are limits to the slowest speed you can select. For instance, if frame rate is 24, 25, or 30, the slowest possible speed is 1/30 sec.

While all these adjustment options are welcome, actually using them while shooting is fiddly. It's difficult to avoid jogging the camera unless it's on a very solid tripod, and the built-in microphone may also pick up the sounds you make as you handle the camera (the Command Dial can sound horrendously loud). Another consequence can be abrupt changes in brightness level in the resulting footage. It's nearly always better to set exposure level before the shot and leave well alone while actually recording a clip.

› Lighting

For obvious reasons, you can't use flash. LED light units specifically designed for DSLR-movie shooting are readily available, and the D500's ability to shoot at high ISO ratings is invaluable.

› Sound

The D3200 has a built-in microphone, giving modest quality mono output. The internal mike is very sensitive to wind noise and is also liable to pick up any sounds you make while operating the camera (focusing, zooming, even breathing). Older lenses may have noisy AF motors, too; AF-S lenses with their Silent Wave motors are much quieter, though still not completely silent. The Movie settings section of the Shooting menu includes the option to turn the microphone off.

Turning it off is logical if you plan to add a new soundtrack later. For a music track or separate, scripted commentary, this is straightforward. However, this is more difficult if you want to record specific ambient sounds, harder still if you want to include people speaking. If you need to include dialog or "talking heads," keep subjects close to the camera and ensure that background noise is minimized. Much the best option is to use a separate microphone such as Nikon's ME-1.

» PREPARATION

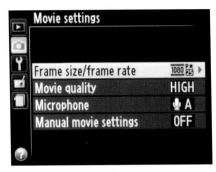

Movie settings section of the Shooting menu.

Before starting to shoot, select key settings in the Movie settings section of the Shooting menu. But before you even do this, check that the Video mode setting (see page 100) in the Setup menu is correct: NTSC in North America and Japan, PAL in most other countries.

Quality options are High or Normal. These can be loosely compared with the JPEG quality options for shooting stills. High-quality files take up more space on memory cards and hard disks but can give better results on critical viewing.

Microphone options are Auto sensitivity, Manual sensitivity and Microphone off. If you select Manual sensitivity, you can set the recording level using ▲ and ▼; there's a live levels display to help you.

Turn Manual movie settings On to allow shutter speed and ISO to be adjusted during shooting in mode M.

Frame size	Frame rate (in Video mode NTSC)	Frame rate (in Video mode PAL)
1920 x 1080 pixels	25	30
	24	24
1280 x 720 pixels	50	60
640 x 424 pixels	25	30

Frame size/frame rate offers the above options.

› Shooting

1) Choose exposure mode, AF mode and AF-area mode as for Live View shooting *(see page 73)*.

2) Activate Live View by pressing the **Lv** button.

3) Check framing and initial exposure level. If using A or M exposure mode, set the aperture. Set initial focus by half-pressure on the shutter-release button.

4) Press O to start recording the movie. A red **REC** flashes at the top of the monitor screen while recording, and an indicator shows the maximum remaining shooting time.

5) To stop recording, press O again.

6) Exit Live View by pressing the **Lv** button.

To take a still photo during movie shooting, press the shutter-release button and keep it pressed until you hear the shutter operate; this can take around a second to happen, so it's utterly hit-and-miss with moving subjects. This ends the recording of the movie clip and returns you to Live View.

» SHOOTING

A golden rule when shooting movies with the D3200, even more than stills, is to think ahead. When shooting stills, you can review a shot, change position or settings, and shoot again within a second or two. To shoot and review even a short movie clip eats up much more time, and often you don't get a second chance anyway. Therefore it's doubly important to make sure shooting position, framing, and camera settings are right before you start. It's easy to check the general look of the shot by shooting a still frame before you start the movie clip; this is a good habit to get into.

However, a still frame does not allow for movement of the subject, the camera, or both. For example, the D3200 has limited ability to follow focus on a moving subject in movie shooting. This can be an issue if your subject is moving towards or away from the camera, or if you plan to pan across a scene which contains objects at a range of different distances. You can sometimes rely on depth of field *(see page 119)* to cope with this, more so when

shooting with wide-angle lenses than long telephotos. Rapid subject movement can be a real problem.

This suggests that it is relatively easy to shoot action when the subject is at a constant distance (e.g. panning shots from the inside of a curve); otherwise, depth of field is your friend, so use a small aperture, with a high ISO setting if necessary.

Shooting movies is a complex business, so start with simple shots; don't try zooming, panning and changing focus simultaneously, but change one thing at a time. Many moving subjects can be filmed with a stationary camera: waterfalls, birds at a feeder, musicians playing, to name but a few. Equally, you can become familiar with camera movement while shooting static subjects: try panning across a wide landscape or zooming in from a broad cityscape to a detail of a single building.

› Handheld or tripod shooting

Shooting movie clips handheld is a good way to reveal just how wobbly you really are—especially as you can't use the viewfinder. Of course even "real" movie directors sometimes use handheld cameras to create a specific feel, but there's a big difference between controlled movement for deliberate effect, and uncontrolled and unending wobble. Using a tripod, or other

> ### Tip
>
> *Still frames can also be extracted from movies but will only be at the image size selected for movie recording.*

suitable camera support, is the easiest way to give movie clips a polished, professional, look. It's true for static shots, and even more so when you start panning or zooming.

Any reasonably solid tripod with a pan-and-tilt head will do to begin with, but if you're serious about movies, consider a dedicated video tripod—the tripod head is specifically designed for smooth movements. You may find that you can keep your existing tripod legs and just replace the head.

If you choose to handhold, or need to shoot a clip with no tripod available, approach it carefully. Pick a spot where you won't be jostled and look for solid support for your elbows, for instance by sitting, with elbows braced on your knees. And "think steady."

Tip

There's now a wide range of devices available to help smooth out movement in the "handheld" camera, from simple brackets to shoulder supports and on up to the famous Steadicam system—though even its base model, the Merlin, costs as much as a D3200 body.

› Panning

The panning shot is a mainstay of movie-making. Often essential for following a moving subject, it can also be used very effectively with static subjects. For instance, a panning shot enables you to capture a

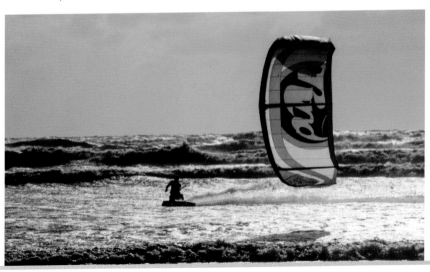

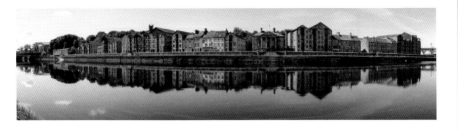

vast panorama in a way that's impossible in a static shot or still frame.

Handheld panning is very problematic: it may be vaguely acceptable when following a moving subject, but a wobbly pan across a grand landscape will definitely annoy viewers. You really, really need a tripod for this—and it needs to be properly leveled, or you may start panning with the camera aimed at the horizon but finish seeing nothing but ground or sky. Many tripods have a built-in spirit level. Failing this, visually check that the tripod's center column looks vertical from all sides. Then do a "dry-run" before shooting.

If you're panning to follow a moving subject you also need to think about the subject's expected path. Some subjects, like trains and trams, move along predictable paths. At the other extreme, trying to follow a player in a soccer match can be very challenging—even seasoned pros don't always get it right.

ON THE LEVEL «
Panning with the surfer is an obvious shot. If using a tripod, make sure it's correctly leveled, or the ocean could appear to be far from level!

PAN-TASTIC ^^
The camera can "explore" a scene like this either by panning across it or by zooming in on specific aspects. (This image was actually produced by "stitching" five still frames.)

Keep panning movements slow and steady. Panning too rapidly can make it hard to "read" the shot and even make the viewer feel seasick. On the D3200 it can also make objects appear distorted (see page 138). Smooth panning is easiest with video tripods, but perfectly possible with a standard model. Leave the pan adjustment slack but make sure the other adjustments are tight. It's probably better to hold the tripod head rather than the camera. Rather than looking at the screen, use the front of the lens as a reference to track steadily across the scene.

With moving subjects, the speed and direction of panning is dictated by the need to keep the subject in frame. Accurate tracking of fast-moving subjects is very challenging and takes a lot of practice.

› Zooming

The zoom is another fundamental movie technique. Moving from a wide view to a tighter one is called *zooming in*, and the converse is *zooming out*. A little forethought makes all the difference to using the zoom effectively; consider which zoom direction you want (in or out), and think about the framing of the shot both at the start and at the finish. If you're zooming in to a specific subject, double-check it's central to the frame before starting.

The D3200 and the range of available lenses are not designed specifically for shooting movies and this shows up clearly when it comes to zooming. Firstly, none of them have such a wide zoom range as video camera lenses, though "superzooms" (e.g. the Nikkor 18–300mm) can be handy for movie shooting. They may lack ultimate quality for still images, but video (even Full HD) has much lower definition. Even so, sometimes you may have to cut from one shot to another instead of linking them in a continuous zoom.

Secondly, it's hard to achieve a totally smooth, even-paced zoom action. Practice does help, and firmly mounting the camera on a solid tripod helps even more. Zooming while handholding virtually guarantees jerky zoom and overall wobbliness. If you have several lenses available, it's worth experimenting to see which has the smoothest zoom action.

When zooming, remember that depth of field *(see page 119)* decreases at the telephoto end of the range. Your subject may appear perfectly sharp in a wide-angle view but end up looking quite fuzzy when you zoom in. If the camera refocuses, the sudden shift in focus is itself a distraction. To avoid this, set focus at the telephoto end of the zoom whether you're starting here and zooming out, or zooming in to end up here. For more on focusing, see below.

› Tracking

The tracking shot, where the camera moves across the setting, is also part of the movie lexicon. With the right rig you can do this by walking but usually a wheeled support is better. Small wheels are much more sensitive to rough surfaces. A bicycle could work well; a tripod sitting inside an old pram might look a bit odd but will do the job.

ZOOMING IN   »
It was necessary to check that the zoom was centered on the statue—zooming into a blank patch of sky or nondescript wall would not have looked good.

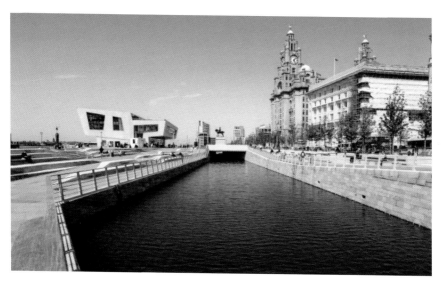

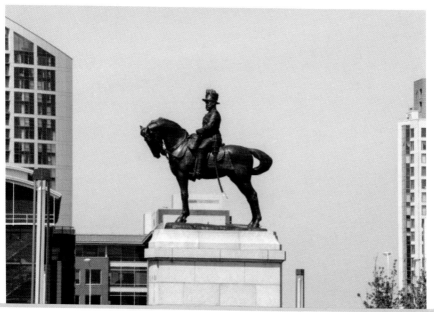

6 » EDITING

Like all movie cameras, the D3200 doesn't shoot movies, it shoots movie clips. A single clip straight from the camera may serve for some purposes (if you capture a bank raid in progress it could even earn you a reward!) but to turn a collection of clips into a movie that people actually want to see requires editing.

The name of the game here is Non-Linear Editing (NLE). This simply means that clips in the final movie don't have to appear in the same order in which they were shot. You might shoot a stunning tropical sunset on the first night of your holiday, but use it as the closing shot in your movie.

In fact, with modern software, editing movies is almost easier to do than it is to describe. The D3200's .AVI movies are a standard format which can be edited in most available programs. Even better, if you own a reasonably recent computer you probably already have suitable software.

› Importing movies to the computer

The basic procedure for importing movies is much the same as for stills *(see page 232)*. Nikon Transfer will recognize and import them, but it's likely you will want to store movies in a different folder than still images. Some dedicated photographic software will not import movie files. Often the best way to import movie files is through your movie-editing software (see below); this ensures that all your movie clips are stored in the same place and that the software can immediately locate them for editing purposes.

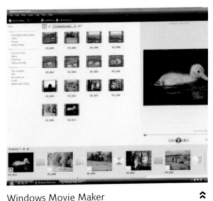

Windows Movie Maker ⌃

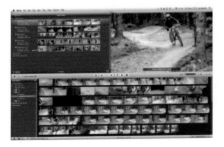

iMovie «

> ## Editing software

For Mac users the obvious choice is Apple's own iMovie, part of the iLife suite, which is included with all new Macs. The Windows equivalent is Windows Movie Maker, which came pre-installed with Windows Vista; for Windows 7 it needs to be downloaded from windowslive.com.

Both programs offer Non-Linear Editing, which is also non-destructive. This just means that editing does not affect your original clips (unlike cutting and splicing bits of film in the "old days"). The new movie is produced by copying desired sections of your clips. In fact, during the editing process you work with preview versions of these clips and the software merely keeps "notes" on the edit; a new movie file is only created when you select Export Movie (in iMovie) or Save (in Windows Movie Maker).

The two programs work in broadly similar ways and both are easy to grasp. iMovie has a largely visual interface, while Windows Movie Maker relies a bit more on text-based menus. In both cases, the movie clips you work with are displayed in one pane of the screen and you simply drag the one you want to the Project pane (iMovie) or Timeline (Windows Movie Maker). You can rearrange clips at any time just by drag-and-drop and you can also trim any clip to a desired length (iMovie's procedure for this is definitely more intuitive). A Viewer pane allows you to preview your movie as a work-in-progress at any time.

In addition, you can adjust the look of any clip or segment of the movie. There are basic controls for brightness, color and so on, just as with any photo-editing program, and a range of special effects can be added: you can, for instance, make your movie look "aged" (scratched and faded), as if it had been shot on film 50 years ago rather than yesterday with a digital SLR.

Another basic feature is the *transition*. This means that instead of simply cutting instantaneously from one shot to the next, you can apply various effects such as dissolves, wipes and fades. They're fun to play with and can add visual polish to the finished movie, but should enhance the shots either side and help the narrative flow of the movie, rather than calling attention to themselves. It's generally

Tip

It's fun to play with special effects, and non-destructive editing means you can experiment to your heart's content, but it's best to use them sparingly in the final version if you want audiences to enjoy rather than endure your movie.

6

better to work with just a few transitions rather than using every possible trick in the course of a five-minute movie.

› Adding to your movie

iMovie and Windows Movie Maker also allow you to add other media to your movie, like still photos and sound.

With a quality camera like the D3200, adding stills is a natural and easy thing to do, but you can use photos from other sources too. You can insert them individually at appropriate points or create slideshows within the main movie. Again various effects and transitions can be applied to give a more dynamic feel as you move from one photo to the next.

It's equally easy to add a new soundtrack, like a voiceover or music, to part or all of the movie.

Last but not least, you can also add titles and captions—perhaps crediting yourself as

Adding titles in iMovie

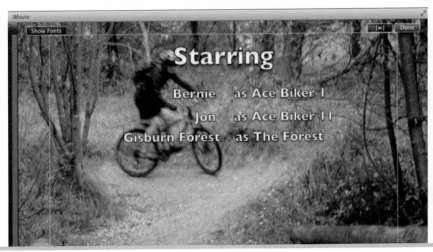

producer, director, camera operator, sound recordist, editor, Best Boy and Key Grip!

› Storyboarding

Editing can transform a jumbled assortment of clips into a coherent movie. But it can also lead to frustration when you start to wish you had a wider shot of "X", or a close-up of "Y". Editing can do a lot, but it can't supply shots you never got in the first place. This is where planning comes in, and this is why big movie productions start with a screenplay, and then go on to create a storyboard, before a single scene is shot. A storyboard usually looks like a giant comic strip, with sketches or mock-ups of every shot and scene that's envisaged in the final movie. Things can still change significantly in the final edit, but storyboarding should mean that director and editor have all the material they need to work with. You may not want to go that far, but a bit of forward-planning can still add massively to the end-product.

HOT DOG ❯❯
With a subject moving as fast as this, keeping the dog central in the frame took real concentration.

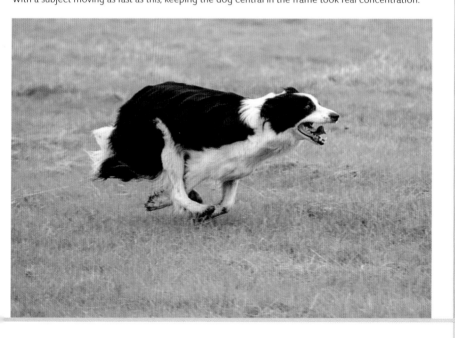

Chapter 7
LENSES

7 LENSES

There are many reasons to choose an SLR like the D3200 rather than a compact. One of the most important is the ability to use a vast range of lenses, including Nikon's own legendary system as well as lenses from other makers. Nikon's F-mount for lenses is now 50 years old, though it has evolved in that time. Still, most Nikkor lenses will fit the D3200, and work (albeit sometimes with major limitations). However, there are still sound reasons why more recent lenses are most suitable, notably that many older lenses cannot autofocus on the D3200 *(see facing page)*.

Another reason for preferring lenses designed specifically for digital cameras relates to the way light reaches the minute individual photodiodes or "photosites" on the camera's sensor. Because these are slightly recessed, there can be some cut-off if light hits them at an angle. This is less critical with film, for which older Nikkor lenses were designed. Many older lenses can still be used, and can give very good results, but critical examination may show some peripheral loss of brightness (vignetting), and perhaps a hint of chromatic aberration (color fringing). Wide-angle lenses are usually most susceptible. Much depends on the size of print or reproduction you require, and these shortcomings can to some extent be corrected in post-processing (especially if you shoot RAW).

Nikon's DX-series and other newer lenses are specifically designed for digital cameras, maintaining illumination and image quality right across the frame. DX lenses are therefore listed first in the table of Nikkor lenses *on page 208.*

Warning!

Some older lenses, specifically pre-AI lenses, should not be used as damage can result. Non-AI lenses can be recognized by their distinctive meter-coupling prong *(see photo on facing page).* Certain other specific (and uncommon) lenses should also be avoided—see the maker's manual.

When older lenses are used on the Nikon D3200, many functions may be lost. In particular, autofocus is only available with lenses with a built-in motor. Suitable Nikon lenses are designated AF-I or AF-S. Check carefully when considering lenses from independent makers (e.g. with Sigma lenses, look for the "HSM" tag).

Other AF lenses with a built-in CPU will support some or all of the camera's metering functions and exposure modes, but will require manual focusing. The electronic rangefinder *(see page 55)* can be helpful for this. The Nikon manual has detailed information on compatible lenses.

Older lenses without a built-in CPU, such as AI and AI-S types, can be attached, but the camera's metering will not operate, requiring you to use exposure mode M. Set aperture and shutter speed using an external meter or simply by trial and error, using the histogram *(see page 83)* as a guide to correct exposure. This may seem a lot of hassle but rarely takes more than half a minute. When using flash or indoor lighting, the same exposure settings can often be repeated again and again, perhaps with minor variations to suit different subjects.

METER COUPLING ⯆
The distinctive meter coupling of an old, pre-AI lens, which should be avoided.

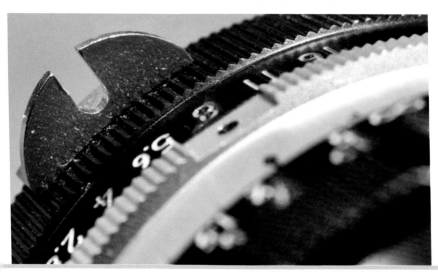

7 » NIKON LENS TECHNOLOGY

Nikon lenses have long been renowned for technical and optical excellence, and many modern lenses incorporate special features or materials. As these are referred to extensively in the table *on page 208*, brief explanations of the main terms and acronyms are given here.

Abbreviation	Term	Explanation
AF	Autofocus	Lens focuses automatically. Most current Nikkor lenses are AF, but a substantial manual-focus range remains.
ASP	Aspherical Lens Elements	Precisely configured lens elements that reduce the incidence of certain aberrations. Especially useful in reducing distortion with wide-angle lenses.
CRC	Close-range Correction	Advanced lens design that improves picture quality at close-focusing distances.
D	Distance information	D-type and G-type lenses communicate information to the camera about the distance at which they are focusing, supporting functions like 3D Matrix Metering.
DC	Defocus-Image Control	Found in a few lenses aimed mostly at portrait photographers; allows control of aberrations and thereby appearance of out-of-focus areas in the image.
DX	DX lens	Lenses designed for DX-format digital cameras *(see page 196)*.
G	G-type lens	Modern Nikkor lenses with no aperture ring; aperture must be set by the camera.
ED	Extra-low Dispersion	ED glass minimizes chromatic aberration (tendency for light of different colors to be focused at different points).
IF	Internal Focusing	Only internal elements of the lens move during focusing: the front element does not extend or rotate.
M/A	Manual/Auto	Many Nikkor AF lenses offer M/A mode, allowing seamless transition from automatic to manual focusing.

Abbreviation	Term	Explanation
N	Nano Crystal Coat	Said to virtually eliminate internal reflections within lenses, minimizing flare.
PC	Perspective Control	*See page 207.*
RF	Rear Focusing	Lens design where only the rearmost elements move during focusing; makes AF operation faster.
SIC	Super Integrated Coating	Nikon-developed lens coating that minimizes flare and "ghosting."
SWM	Silent Wave Motor	Special in-lens motors that deliver very fast and very quiet autofocus operation.
VR	Vibration Reduction	System which compensates for camera shake. VR is said to allow handheld shooting up to three stops slower than would otherwise be possible (i.e. 1/15 instead of 1/125 sec.). New lenses feature VRII, said to gain an extra stop over VR (1/8 instead of 1/125 sec.).

⇢ FOCAL LENGTH

Though familiar, the term "focal length" is often misapplied. The focal length of any lens is a fundamental optical property, and is not changed by fitting the lens to a different camera. Unfortunately, as if to promote confusion, the lenses on most digital compact cameras are described not by their actual focal length but by their "35mm equivalent"—i.e. the focal length that would give the same angle of view on a 35mm or full-frame camera. Of course, zoom lenses have variable focal length— that's what zoom means—but an 18–55mm zoom is always an 18–55 zoom, regardless of whether it's fitted on a DX-format camera like the D3200 or a full-frame (FX) camera like the D800. However, because the D3200 has a smaller sensor than the D800, the actual image has a smaller angle of view.

7 › Crop factor

The D3200's smaller sensor, relative to the 35mm/FX standard, gives it a **crop factor**, also referred to as **focal length magnification factor**, of 1.5. If you fit a 200mm lens to a D3200, the field of view equates to what you'd see with a 300mm lens on a full-frame camera (e.g. D4 or D800). For sports and wildlife this can be an advantage, allowing long-range shooting with relatively light and inexpensive lenses. Conversely, the crop factor makes wide-angle lenses effectively less wide, which is unwelcome for landscape shooters. However, this has fostered the development of new ultra-wide lenses, like the 10–24mm f/3.5–4.5G DX Nikkor.

The next page shows a series of images taken on a Nikon D3200, from a fixed position, with lenses from 14mm to 300mm.

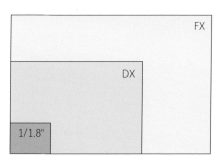

CROP FACTOR   ⌃
Comparison chart of digital camera sensor sizes.

› Field of view

The field of view, or angle of view, is the area covered by the image frame. While the focal length of a lens remains the same on any camera, the angle of view seen in the image is different for different sensor formats. The angle of view is usually measured diagonally *(as in the table on page 208).*

PICK OF THE CROP   »
The opposite page shows a series of images taken on a Nikon D3200, from a fixed position, with lenses from 14mm to 300mm. *Focal lengths as shown, 1/250 sec., f/10, ISO 200.*

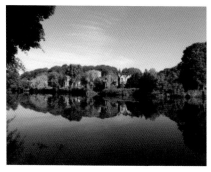

14mm

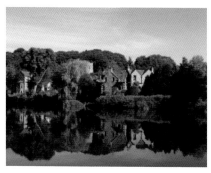

28mm

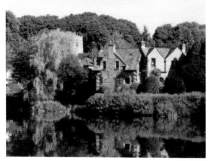

50mm

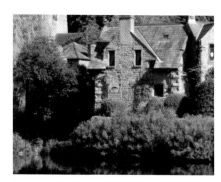

100mm

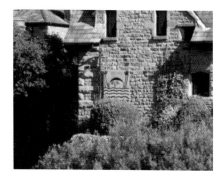

200mm

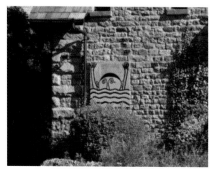

300mm

7 » PERSPECTIVE

Perspective concerns the visual relationship between objects at different distances. The apparent fading of distant objects due to haze is atmospheric perspective, while optical perspective relates to the changes in apparent size of objects at different distances.

It's commonly asserted that different lenses give different perspective. This is wrong: perspective is determined solely by distance. However, different lenses do lend themselves to different working distances and therefore are often associated with different perspective.

A powerful emphasis on the foreground may be loosely called "wide-angle perspective" because a wide-angle lens allows you to move closer to foreground objects. Similarly, the apparent compression of perspective in telephoto shots is a result of the greater working distance associated with the long lens. In the series of shots facing, the gantry remains the same apparent size even though it's viewed from different distances, but both its apparent shape and its relationship to the background are altered.

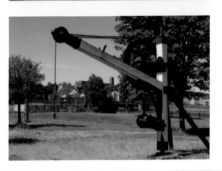

IN PERSPECTIVE   « ⌄
Focal length 95mm, approximate distance 20m *(left)*; focal length 34mm, approximate distance 8m *(bottom left)*; focal length 14mm, approximate distance 2m *(below)*.

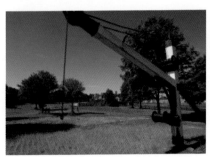

» PRIME LENSES

Prime lenses have a fixed focal length (no zoom function). This makes them relatively light and simple. They are also usually optically excellent and have wide maximum apertures. They may appear less versatile than zoom lenses but this can be a good lesson, making the photographer shift position rather than lazily twiddling a zoom.

TIME TO REFLECT   ⌄
A fixed standard lens can force the photographer to view a scene creatively.
32mm, 1/250 sec., f/10, ISO 200.

» STANDARD LENSES

In traditional 35mm film photography, a 50mm lens was called standard, as its field of view was held to approximate that of the human eye. Because of the crop factor of the D3200, the equivalent lens is around 35mm. Standard lenses are typically light, simple and have wide maximum apertures. Zoom lenses encompassing this focal length are often referred to as "standard zooms."

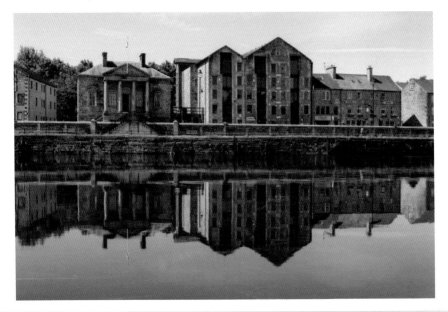

7 » WIDE-ANGLE LENSES

A wide-angle lens is any lens with a wider view than a standard lens; for the D3200 this means any lens shorter than 35mm. Wide-angle lenses are valuable for working close to subjects or emphasizing foregrounds. They excel in photographing expansive scenic views, and also in cramped spaces where you can't step back to "get more in."

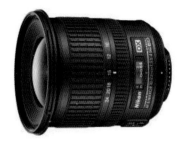

Nikkor 10–24mm f/3.5–4.5G ED AF-S DX

NEAR AND WIDE ⌄
Wide-angle lenses can distort the elements of the scene that are closer to the lens, but they provide a "big picture" view. *13mm, 1/200 sec., f/14, ISO 200.*

» TELEPHOTO LENSES

Telephoto lenses, or simply "long" lenses, give a narrow angle of view. They are commonly employed in wildlife and sports photography, where working distances are often great, but can also isolate small or distant elements in a landscape. Moderate telephoto lenses are favored for portrait photography, because a greater working distance is felt to give a natural-looking result, and is less intimidating for nervous subjects. The traditional "portrait" range is 85–135mm, equivalent to 60–90mm with the D3200.

The laws of optics, plus greater working distance, mean telephoto lenses produce limited depth of field. This is often welcomed in portraiture, wildlife and sport, as it concentrates attention on the subject by throwing backgrounds out of focus.

The size and weight of longer lenses

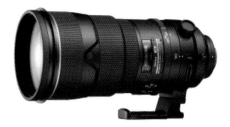

Nikkor 300mm f/4D ED-IF AF-S

> ### Tip
>
> *Switch VR OFF when using the camera on a tripod.*

make them hard to handhold comfortably, and their narrow view also magnifies any movement—high shutter speeds and/or a tripod or other camera support are often required. Nikon's Vibration Reduction (VR) technology also mitigates camera shake.

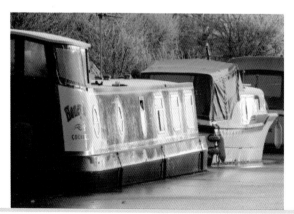

ZOOMING IN　　　　**«**
Telephotos are not just for sports or wildlife photography; they can be used to pick out details in a landscape. *185mm, 1/80 sec., f/11, ISO 200.*

7 » ZOOM LENSES

The term "zoom" covers lenses with variable focal length, like the AF-S DX Nikkor 18-105mm f/3.5-5.6G. A zoom lens can replace a bagful of prime lenses and cover the gaps in between, scoring highly for weight, convenience and economy. Flexible focal length also allows very precise framing.

While once considered inferior in optical quality, there is now little to choose between a good zoom and a good prime

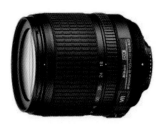

Nikkor 18-105mm F/3.5-5.6G ED VR AF-S DX

lens. Cheaper zooms, and those with a very wide range (e.g. 18-200mm or 28-300mm) may still be optically compromised, and usually have a relatively small ("slow") maximum aperture, but prove useful for movie shooting in particular.

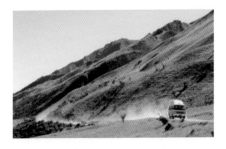

ON THE ROAD 《

Zoom lenses are particularly useful for travel photography. *46mm, 1/320 sec., f/11, ISO 400.*

» MACRO LENSES

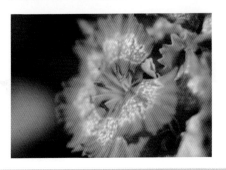

For specialist close-up work there is little to beat a true macro lens. For more on these *see page 173.*

CLOSE WORKING 《

True macro lenses can provide real 1:1 images of stunning detail and quality. *50mm, 1/800 sec., f/5.6, ISO 200.*

» PERSPECTIVE-CONTROL LENSES

Perspective-control ("tilt and shift") lenses give unique flexibility in viewing and controlling the image. Their most obvious application is in photographing architecture, where with a "normal" lens it often becomes necessary to tilt the camera upwards, resulting in converging verticals (buildings appear to lean back or even to one side). The shift function allows the camera back to be kept vertical, which in turn means that vertical lines in the subject remain vertical in the image. Tilt movements also allow extra control over depth of field, whether to extend or to minimize it. The current Nikon range

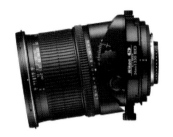

Nikkor 24mm f/3.5D ED PC-E

features three PC lenses, with focal lengths of 24mm, 45mm and 85mm. They retain many automatic functions, but require manual focusing.

» TELECONVERTERS

Teleconverters are supplementary optics which fit between the main lens and the camera body, and magnify the focal length of the main lens. Nikon currently offers the TC-14E II (1.4x magnification), TC-17E II (1.7x) and TC-20E II (2x). The advantages are obvious, allowing you to extend the focal length range with minimal additional weight (the TC-14E II, for example, weighs just 200 grams). However, teleconverters can marginally degrade image quality, and they also cause a loss of light. Fitting a 2x converter to a 300mm f/4 lens turns it into a 600mm f/8, but the camera's autofocus may become very slow or not work at all.

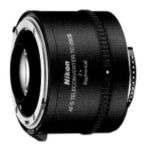

Nikkor AF-S Teleconverter TC-20E III

Warning!

Some recent lenses are incompatible with these teleconverters. Check carefully before use.

7 » NIKKOR LENS CHART

This table lists currently available Nikon autofocus lenses, starting with the DX series, which is specifically designed for DX-format cameras like the D3200.

Optical features/notes

DX Lenses

Lens	
10.5mm f/2.8G DX Fisheye	CRC
10–24mm f/3.5–4.5G ED AF-S DX	ED, IF, SWM
12–24mm f/4G ED-IF AF-S DX	SWM
16–85mm f/3.5–5.6G ED VR AF-S DX	VRII, SWM
17–55mm f/2.8G ED-IF AF-S DX	ED, SWM
18–55mm f/3.5–5.6G AF-S VR DX	VR, SWM
18–55 f/3.5–5.6GII AF-S DX	ED, SWM
18–70mm f3.5–4.5G ED-IF AF-S DX	ED, SWM
18–105mm F/3.5–5.6G ED VR AF-S DX	ED, IF, VRII, NC, SWM
18–200mm f/3.5–5.6G ED AF-S VRII DX	ED, SWM, VRII
18–300mm f/3.5–5.6G ED VR AF-S DX	ED, IF, VRII, SWM
35mm f/1.8G AF-S	SWM
40mm f/2.8G AF-S DX Micro NIKKOR	SWM
55–200mm f/4–5.6 AF-S VR DX	ED, SWM, VR
55–200mm f/4–5.6G ED AF-S DX	ED, SWM
55–300mm f/4.5–5.6G ED VR	ED, SWM
85mm f/3.5G ED VR AF-S DX Micro Nikkor	ED, IF, SWM, VRII

AF Prime lenses

Lens	
14mm f/2.8D ED AF	ED, RF
16mm f/2.8D AF Fisheye	CRC
20mm f/2.8D AF	CRC
24mm f/1.4G ED	ED, NC
24mm f/2.8D AF	
28mm f/1.8G AF-S	NC, SWM

Angle of view on DX format (°)	Min. focus distance (m)	Filter size (mm)	Dimensions dia. x length (mm)	Weight (g)
180	0.14	Rear	63 x 62.5	300
109–61	0.24	77	82.5 x 87	460
99–61	0.3	77	82.5 x 90	485
83–18.5	0.38	67	72 x 85	485
79–28.5	0.36	77	85.5 x 11.5	755
76–28.5	0.28	52	73 x 79.5	265
76–28.5	0.28	52	70.5 x 74	205
76–22.5	0.38	67	73 x 75.5	420
76–15.3	0.45	67	76 x 89	420
76–8	0.5	72	77 x 96.5	560
76–5.3	0.45	77	83 x 120	830
44	0.3	52	70 x 52.5	210
38.5	0.163	52	68.5 x 64.5	235
28.5–8	1.1	52	73 x 99.5	335
28.5–8	0.95	52	68 x 79	255
28.5–5.2	1.4	58	76.5 x 123	530
18.5	0.28	52	73 x 98.5	355
90	0.2	Rear	87 x 86.5	670
120	0.25	Rear	63 x 57	290
70	0.25	62	69 x 42.5	270
61	0.25	77	83 x 88.5	620
61	0.3	52	64.5 x 46	270
53	0.25	67	73 x 80.5	330

7

Optical features/notes

Lens	Notes
28mm f/2.8D AF	
35mm f/2D AF	
35mm f/1.4G AF-S	NC, SWM
50mm f/1.8G AF-S	SWM
50mm f/1.8D AF	
50mm f/1.4D AF	
50mm f/1.4G AF-S	IF, SWM
85mm f/1.4G AF	SWM, NC
85mm f/1.8D AF	RF
85mm f/1.8G AF-S	IF, SWM
105mm f/2D AF DC	DC
135mm f/2D AF DC	DC
180mm f/2.8D ED-IF AF	ED, IF
200mm f/2G ED-IF AF-S VRII	ED, VRII, SWM
300mm f/4D ED-IF AF-S	ED, IF
300mm f/2.8G ED VR II AF-S	ED, VRII, NC, SWM
400mm f/2.8G ED VR AF-S	ED, IF, VRII, NC
400mm f/2.8D ED-IF AF-S II	ED, SWM
500mm f/4G ED VR AF-S	IF, ED, VRII, NC
600mm f/4G ED VR AF-S	ED, IF, VRII, NC

AF Zoom lenses

Lens	Notes
14–24mm f/2.8G ED AF-S	IF, ED, SWM, NC
16–35mm f/4G ED VR	NC, ED, VR
17–35mm f/2.8D ED-IF AF-S	IF, ED, SWM
24–70mm f/2.8G ED AF-S	ED, SWM, NC

Angle of view on DX format (°)	Min. focus distance (m)	Filter size (mm)	Dimensions dia. x length (mm)	Weight (g)
53	0.25	52	65 x 44.5	205
44	0.25	52	64.5 x 43.5	205
44	0.3	67	83 x 89.5	600
31.3	0.45	58	72 x 52.5	185
31.3	0.45	52	63 x 39	160
31.3	0.45	52	64.5 x 42.5	230
31.3	0.45	58	73.5 x 54	280
18.5	0.85	77	86.5 x 84	595
18.5	0.85	62	71.5 x 58.5	380
18.5	0.8	67	80 x 73	350
15.2	0.9	72	79 x 111	640
12	1.1	72	79 x 120	815
9.1	1.5	72	78.5 x 144	760
8.2	1.9	52	124 x 203	2930
5.2	1.45	77	90 x 222.5	1440
5.2	2.2	52	124 x 267.5	2900
4	2.9	52	159.5 x 368	4620
4	3.8	52	160 x 352	4800
3.1	4	52	139.5 x 391	3880
2.4	5	52	166 x 445	5060
90–61	0.28	None	98 x 131.5	970
79–44	0.28	77	82.5 x 106	745
61–22.50	0.38	77	83 x 133	900

Optical features/notes

24–85mm f/2.8–4D IF AF	
24–85mm f/3.5–4.5G ED VR AF-S	ED, VRII, SWM
24–120mm f/4G ED-IF AF-S VR	ED, SWM, NC, VRII
28–300mm f/3.5–5.6G ED VR	ED, SWM
70–200mm f/2.8G ED-IF AF-S VRII	ED, SWM, VRII
70–300mm f/4.5–5.6G AF-S VR	ED, IF, SWM, VRII
80–400mm f/4.5–5.6D ED VR AF	ED, VR
200–400mm f/4G ED-IF AF-S VRII	ED, NC, VRII, SWM

Macro lenses

60mm f/2.8G ED AF-S Micro	ED, SWM, NC
105mm f/2.8G AF-S VR Micro	ED, IF, VRII, NC, SWM
200mm f/4D ED-IF AF Micro	ED, CRC

Perspective control

24mm f/3.5D ED PC-E (manual focus)	ED, NC
45mm f/2.8D ED PC-E (manual focus)	ED, NC
85mm f/2.8D ED PC-E (manual focus)	ED, NC

Angle of view on DX format (°)	Min. focus distance (m)	Filter size (mm)	Dimensions dia. x length (mm)	Weight (g)
61–18.5	0.5	72	78.5 x 82.5	545
61–18.5	0.38	72	78 x 82	465
61–13.5	0.45	77	84 x 103.5	710
53–5.2	0.5	77		800
22.5–8	1.4	77	87 x 209	1540
22.5–5.20		67	80 x 143.5	745
20–4	2.3	77	91 x 171	1340
8–4	2	52	124 x 365.5	3360
26.3	0.185	62	73 x 89	425
15	0.31	62	83 x 116	720
8	0.5	62	76 x 104.5	1190
56	0.21	77	82.5 x 108	730
34.5	0.25	77 x 94	83.5 x 112	780
18.9	0.39	77	82.7 x 107	650

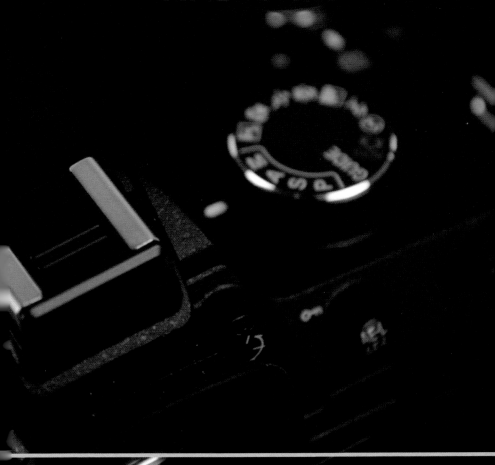

Chapter 8
ACCESSORIES AND CARE

8 ACCESSORIES

As part of the vast Nikon system, a wide choice of accessories is available for the D3200. Third-party items extend the options still further. Accessories can be grouped under four main headings: image modification (e.g. filters and flash); camera performance; camera support; and storage.

» FILTERS

Flash and close-up accessories have already been covered *(see pages 160 and 173)*, leaving filters as the other main category for image modification. As a general principle, avoid using filters unnecessarily. Adding extra layers of glass in front of the lens can increase flare or otherwise degrade the image. "Stacking" of multiple filters increases this risk, and that of vignetting *(see page 140)*.

Some types of filter are almost redundant with digital cameras. Variable white balance, for instance *(see page 63)*, has virtually eliminated the need for color-correction filters, essential for accurate color on film. However, it's prudent to keep a UV or skylight filter (see below) attached to each lens as a defence against knocks and scratches. Filters are much cheaper to replace than lenses!

› Types of filter

Filters can attach to the lens in several ways: round, screw-in filters are the commonest, but you may also encounter slot-in filters and rear or drop-in filters. Screw-in filters are normally made of high-quality optical glass. The filter-thread diameter (in mm) of most Nikon lenses is specified in the table on *page 208*, and usually marked somewhere on the lens beside a Ø symbol. Nikon produces screw-in filters in sizes matching the range of Nikkor lenses and to the same high optical standards. Larger ranges come from Hoya and B+W. Slot-in filters are more economical and convenient if you use filters extensively. The filters—square or rectangular and made of optical resin or gelatin—fit into a slotted holder. With a simple adapter ring for each lens, one holder and one set of filters can serve any number of lenses. The best-known maker is Cokin, while the Lee Filters range is respected by the most demanding users.

A few specialist lenses, such as super-telephotos with huge front diameters, or extreme wide-angle and fish-eye lenses with protruding front elements, require equally specialist filters on the rear of the lens or dropping in a slot in the lens barrel.

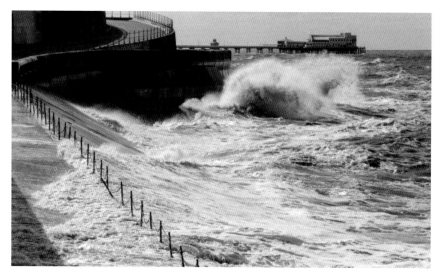

PROTECTION FROM THE ELEMENTS
A UV or skylight filter helps to protect the lens from spray, dust, dirt and other hazards—though, if the risk is serious, the entire outfit should be protected. *86mm, 1/500 sec., f/13, ISO 200.*

› UV and skylight filters

These filters are almost interchangeable. Both cut out excess ultraviolet light which can make images appear excessively cool and blue. The skylight filter also has a slight warming effect. A major benefit is in protecting the front element of the lens.

› Polarizing filters

The polarizing filter, much-loved by landscape photographers, cuts down reflections from most surfaces, intensifying colors in rocks and vegetation, for

instance. It can make reflections on water and glass virtually disappear, restoring transparency—this is most effective at an angle of around 30 degrees to the surface. Rotating the filter in its mount strengthens or weakens its effect.

The polarizer can also "cut through" atmospheric haze (though not mist or fog) like nothing else, and can make blue skies appear more intense. The effect is strongest when shooting at right angles to the direction of the sunlight, vanishing when the sun is directly behind or in front. Results can sometimes appear unnatural. With wide-angle lenses the effect can be

8

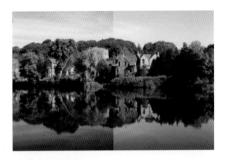

POLAR MOMENT ⌃

A polarizing filter can intensify colors (left side of image). *28mm, 1/40 and 1/160 sec., f/11, ISO 200.*

conspicuously uneven across the field of view. The polarizer should be used with discrimination, not permanently attached. However, many of its effects cannot be fully replicated in any other way, even in digital post-processing. You may only use it occasionally, but then it can be priceless.

› Neutral density filters

Neutral density (ND) filters reduce the amount of light reaching the lens. "Neutral" simply means that they don't affect the color of the light, only its intensity. ND filters can be either plain or graduated.

A plain ND filter is useful when you want to set a slower shutter speed and/or wider aperture, and the ISO setting is already as low as it can go. A classic example is when shooting waterfalls, where a long shutter speed is often favored to create a silky blur.

Graduated ND filters ("grads") have neutral density over half their area, with the other half being clear, and a gradual transition in the middle. They are widely used in landscape photography to compensate for wide differences in brightness between sky and land. However the straight transition of an ND grad filter is unpleasantly obvious when the skyline is irregular, as in mountainous areas.

If you're happy to invest time at the computer you can often replicate, and even improve on, the effect of a graduated ND filter. However, this can't work unless the original image captures detail in both highlights and shadows, so an ND grad is still an important standby; it can also be useful when shooting movies, where this sort of postprocessing is not an option.

› Special-effects filters

Special-effects filters come in many forms, but two common types are soft-focus filters and starburst filters. The soft-focus filter is widely used in portrait photography to soften skin blemishes, but its effects can be replicated and extended, precisely and reversibly, in digital post-processing. Much the same is true of the starburst, and most other special-effects filters. It's usually better to capture the original image "straight", without filters, and apply effects later. That way you can always change your mind.

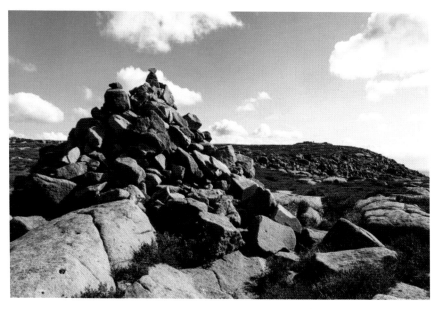

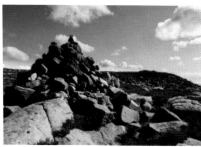

POST CAPTURE TREATMENT   « ☆

There was a big difference in brightness between sky and foreground. A graduated filter offered a crude solution (left: note how it darkens the top of the cairn). For a more subtle result two separate RAW conversions were combined using Photoshop Layer Masks (above). *18mm, 1/125 sec., f/11, ISO 100.*

> ### Tip
>
> *The **Filter effects** section of the Retouch menu (see page 110), mimics the effects of several common photographic filters, including **Skylight**, **Warm filter** and **Cross screen** (starburst).*

8 » CAMERA PERFORMANCE: ESSENTIALS

Numerous add-ons are available to improve or modify the performance of the D3200. Nikon includes several items in the box with the camera, but these are really essentials, not extras.

› EN-EL14 battery

Without a live battery, your D3200 becomes useless dead-weight. It's always wise to have a fully charged spare on hand—especially in cold conditions, when using the screen extensively, or when shooting movies.

› MH-24 charger

Vital to keep the EN-EL14 battery charged and ready.

› BF-1A body cap

Keeps the interior of the camera free of dust and dirt when no lens is attached.

» CAMERA PERFORMANCE: OPTIONAL EXTRAS

Key items from Nikon's extensive range are listed here.

› AC Adapter EH-5a/EH-5

Either of these adapters can be used to power the camera directly from the AC mains, allowing uninterrupted shooting in, for example, long studio sessions. (A Power Connector EP-5 is also required.)

› Wireless remote control ML-L3

This inexpensive little unit allows the camera to be triggered from a distance of up to 16ft (5m).

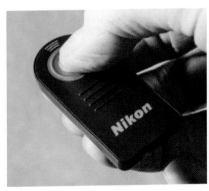

Wireless remote control ML-L3

› WU-1a Wireless Mobile Adapter

The WU-1a Wireless Mobile Adapter plugs into the camera's USB port and connects wirelessly to a suitable smartphone or tablet. You can use this connection to transfer photos and movies, install firmware updates *(see page 106)*, or even control the D3200 remotely. Unfortunately, it's only compatible with Android devices—at least for the moment. An Eye-Fi card *(see page 235)* will let you transfer photos and movies to an iPad, laptop or desktop computer, but won't support the other functions.

› Remote Cord MC-DC2

Nikon's 3ft- (1m-) long MC-DC2 remote cord can be attached to the terminal on the left side of the D3200, allowing shutter release without touching the camera.

› GPS Unit GP-1

A dedicated Global Positioning System device *(see page 106)*.

› ME-1 stereo microphone

Greatly improves sound quality in movie shooting *(see page 183)*.

Tip

It's usually easier to wear contact lenses or glasses. My prescription is around -5 m^{-1} and I've never had any problem using the D3200 while wearing contacts.

› Diopter adjustment

The D3200's viewfinder has built-in dioptric adjustment *(see page 26)*. If your eyesight is outside its range, Nikon produces a series of viewfinder lenses between -5 and $+3$ m^{-1}, with the designation DK-20C.

› Screen shades

The LCD screen can be impossible to see properly in bright sunlight—this can be a real issue when using Live View and even more for shooting movies. Various third-party companies produce accessory screen shades; one of the best-known names is Hoodman. However, if you only need one occasionally, a screen shade can be improvized; we have heard of people using the cardboard core from a toilet roll!

8 » CAMERA SUPPORT

There's much more to camera support than tripods, although these remain a staple.

› Tripods

VR lenses, plus the D3200's ability to produce good-quality images at high-ISO settings, do encourage handholding, but there are still many occasions where nothing replaces a tripod. While light weight and low cost always appeal, beware of flimsy tripods that just aren't sturdy enough to provide decent support, especially with longer lenses. A good tripod is an investment that should last many years. The best combination of low weight with good rigidity comes in titanium or carbon fiber, though these tripods can cost as much as the camera. Carbon fiber tripods are made by Manfrotto and Gitzo, among others. The unusual design of the Benbo range of tripods gives them great flexibility and they are popular with nature photographers for shooting in awkward positions.

When shooting movies, a tripod is essential, and many tripods and heads are designed specifically for this purpose *(see page 185).*

› Monopods

Monopods can't equal the ultimate stability of a tripod, but are light, easy to carry and quick to set up. They are favored by sports photographers, who have to react quickly while using hefty long telephoto lenses.

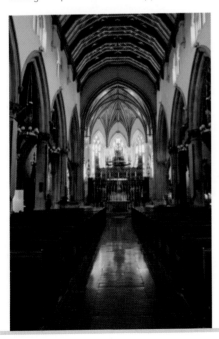

LOW-LIGHT SUPPORT 《
Tripods are ideal for a wide variety of subjects, whether it's to deal with low light, support long lenses or to aid in considered framing. *18mm, 15 sec., f/16, ISO 100.*

› Other camera support

There are many other solutions for camera support, both proprietary products and improvized alternatives. It's still hard to beat the humble beanbag; these can be home-made, or bought from various suppliers. For movie-specific camera support *see page 186*.

BAG OF BEANS ⨯
This simple, homemade beanbag has served me well for many years.

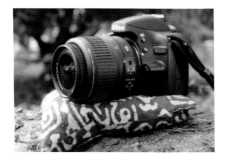

> ### *Tip*
>
> *SD cards are tiny and easily mislaid. Though robust, they may not survive being trodden on or dropped into water. Cards loaded with irreplaceable images should be stored securely in the safest possible place.*

› Memory cards

The D3200 stores images on Secure Digital (SD), SDHC and SDXC cards. On long trips it's easy to fill up even large-capacity memory cards and they are now remarkably cheap, so it's advisable to carry a spare or two. Fast card-write speeds accelerate the camera's operation and are important for movie shooting.

› Portable storage devices

Memory cards rarely fail but it's always worth backing up valuable images as soon as possible. Many photographers use some sort of mobile device. Dedicated photo storage devices comprise a compact hard drive along with a small screen; prominent makers include Vosonic, Epson and Jobo. However many of us already own something that will also store images, in the shape of an iPod. Not all iPod models are suitable, so investigate carefully. The iPad (but not the iPhone) also works well for this; you'll need an Apple iPad Camera Connector.

8 CARE

The Nikon D3200 is a solid, well-made camera, but it is still packed with highly complex electronic and optical technology, which can be vulnerable to damage. A few simple, and generally commonsensical, precautions should ensure that it keeps functioning perfectly for many years.

» BASIC CARE

Keeping the camera clean is fundamental. The camera body can be cleaned by removing dust and dirt with a blower, then wiping with a soft, dry cloth. After exposure to salt spray, wipe carefully with a cloth lightly dampened with clean water (ideally distilled or de-ionized water), then dry thoroughly. As prevention is better than cure, keep the camera in a case when not in use.

Lenses require special care. Glass elements and coatings are easily scratched and this will degrade your images. Remove dust and dirt with a blower. Fingerprints and other marks should be removed using a dedicated lens cleaner and optical-grade cloth. Again, prevention is better than cure, so use a skylight or UV filter to protect the lens, and lens caps should be replaced when the lens is not in use.

Warning!

The Nikon Reference manual (supplied on the CD, p179) seems to imply that the reflex mirror can be cleaned with a soft cloth and lens cleaning fluid. This goes against all advice from every other source. Never touch the reflex mirror in any way, as its coating is very delicate, and the mirror itself can easily be misaligned, with dire consequences for viewing and focusing. Remove dust from the mirror with gentle use of an air-blower. Take great care during this process, and at all other times, not to touch the mirror.

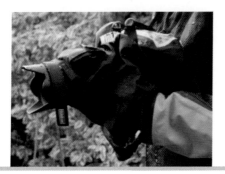

GET IT COVERED **«**
A very effective raincover, specifically designed for a professional 70–200 f/2.8 zoom lens.

› Screen care

The LCD monitor is central to the way you interact with the camera, as most settings can only be viewed and changed there. It's also where you review the shots you've taken. While there's no need to touch the screen with your fingers, it does tend to come into contact with your nose when you're using the viewfinder. If you carry the camera round your neck the screen will bounce and swing against with your clothes. Beware of buttons, zips and other hard objects that could scratch the screen.

Nikon does not supply a screen protector with the D3200 but third-party suppliers do produce a variety of suitable screen protectors, and one of these would be a sound investment.

When the screen needs cleaning, use a blower to remove loose dirt, then wipe the surface carefully with a clean soft cloth. Do not apply pressure and do not use water or chemical cleaners.

Warning!

Never use household cleaning products on or near the camera.

› Storage

If the camera is to go unused for any length of time, remove the battery, close the battery compartment cover and store in a cool, dry place. Avoid extremes of temperature, high humidity, and strong electromagnetic fields such as those produced by TV and computer equipment.

› Cleaning the sensor

To speak of sensor cleaning is slightly misleading as the sensor itself is protected by a low-pass filter (see page 100). Specks of dust and dirt settling on this will appear as dark spots or smears in the image. Prevention is better than cure (see page 228) but unless you never change lenses, some dust will eventually find its way in.

Fortunately, the D3200 is well-equipped to keep dust at bay. Its Airflow control system minimizes dust settling on the sensor in the first place, while automated sensor cleaning (see page 100) usually shifts most of it. These measures greatly reduce the occurrence of dust spots and the need for invasive cleaning—very welcome if you've experienced them!

Occasionally, however, stubborn spots may still appear on the low-pass filter, and it then becomes necessary to clean it by hand. This requires a clean, draught-free

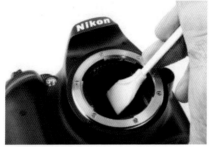

SENSITIVE BRUSH ☆
Cleaning the sensor is strictly for the confident!

Warning!

Any damage to the low-pass filter from incorrect use of a cleaning swab could void your warranty. If in doubt, consult a professional dealer or camera repairer.

Tip

If, despite your best efforts, spots do appear on the image, they can always be removed using, for example, the Clone tool or Healing brush in Adobe Photoshop. In Nikon Capture NX2 this process can be automated by creating a Dust-off reference image (see page 102). Spot-removal can be applied across batches of images in Adobe Lightroom.

area with good light, preferably using a lamp which can be directed (from a safe distance) into the camera's interior. Some systems include magnifiers which allow close inspection of the low-pass filter, as well as dedicated cleaning swabs.

Make sure the battery is fully charged or use a mains adapter if you have one. Remove the lens, switch the camera ON and select Lock mirror up for cleaning from the Setup menu. Press the shutter-release button to lock up the mirror. First, attempt to remove dust using a hand-blower (not compressed air or other aerosol). If this appears ineffective, consider using a dedicated sensor cleaning swab, and carefully follow the instructions supplied with it. Do not use other brushes or cloths and never touch the low-pass filter with your finger. The filter is very delicate (and the sensor itself even more so). When cleaning is complete, turn the camera OFF and the mirror will reset.

› **Coping with cold**

Nikon specify an operating temperature range of 32–104°F (0–40°C). This does not mean that the camera cannot be used when the temperature is below freezing, but as far as possible the camera itself should be kept within the stated range. Keeping the camera in an insulated case or under outer layers of clothing between shots will help to keep it warmer than the surroundings, but don't put it too near your skin as condensation can become a problem. If it does become chilled, battery life may be severely reduced. In extreme cold, the LCD display may become erratic or disappear completely and ultimately the camera may stop working altogether. If allowed to warm up gently, no permanent harm should result.

FROST BITES   ⌄
Frosty weather offers lots of great picture potential, but can prove challenging for the camera. *80mm, 1/200 sec., f/11, ISO 400.*

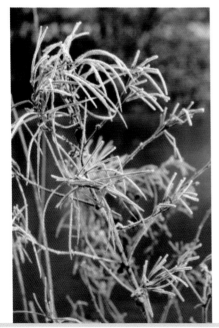

› Coping with heat and humidity

Extremes of heat, and especially humidity (Nikon stipulate over 85%), can be even more problematic, and are more likely to lead to long-term damage. In particular, rapid transfers from cool environments (say an aircraft cabin) to hot and humid ones (the streets of Bangkok) can lead to condensation within the lens and camera. If you anticipate such a transition, pack the camera and lens(es) in airtight containers with sachets of silica gel, which absorbs moisture. Allow equipment to reach the ambient temperature before unpacking and using it.

› Water protection

The D3200 does not claim to be waterproof, but brief exposure to light rain is unlikely to do permanent harm. Exposure should be minimized, and the camera wiped regularly with a microfiber cloth. A cloth of this kind is always handy to wipe off any accidental splashes. Avoid using the built-in flash if it's raining or splashing is likely. The hotshoe cover should also be in place (this is one of the easiest things to lose!). Double-check that all access covers on the camera are properly closed.

Salt water is particularly hostile to electronic components, so take extra care to avoid any contact. If this does occur, clean carefully and immediately with a

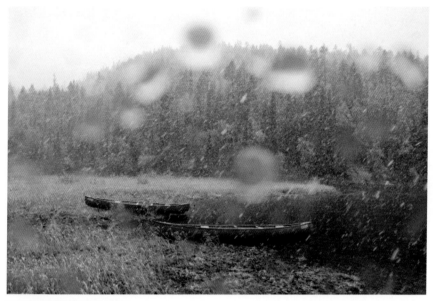

RAINDROPS KEEP FALLING ⌃
A clear need for water protection! Drops need
wiping from the lens cover before each shot to
avoid this kind of blobby result.

cloth lightly dampened with fresh water,
or preferably distilled or deionized water.

Ideally, protect the camera with a
waterproof cover. A simple plastic bag will
provide reasonable protection, but
purpose-made rain-guards are available,
e.g. from Think Tank Photo. True
waterproof cases like the Aquapac range
provide complete protection, but when
used above the water-surface splashes on
the lens glass can be very obvious.

› Dust protection

To minimize any entry of dust into the
camera, take great care when changing
lenses. Aim the camera slightly downward
and stand with your back to any wind. In
really bad conditions (such as sandstorms)
it's best not to change lenses at all, and
better still to protect the camera with a
waterproof, and therefore also dust-proof,
case. Dust that settles on the outside of the
camera is relatively easy to remove—the

safest way is with a hand-operated or compressed-air blower. Do this before changing lenses, memory cards or batteries.

› Camera cases

In all conditions, some sort of case is highly advisable to protect the camera when not in use. The most practical is a simple drop-in pouch which can be worn on a waist-belt. Excellent examples come from makers like Think Tank Photo, Camera Care Systems and LowePro.

› Card care

If a memory card is lost or damaged, your images are lost too. Blank cards are cheap but cards full of images can be irreplaceable—unlike the camera itself. As SD cards use solid-state memory, they are pretty robust but it's still wise to treat them with care. Keep them in their original plastic cases, or something more robust, and avoid exposure to extremes of temperature, direct sunlight, liquids, and strong electromagnetic fields.

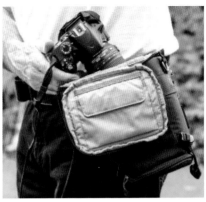

IN THE BAG ⌃
A padded pouch combines good protection and easy access.

Note:
There seems to be no evidence that modern airport X-ray machines have any harmful effect on either digital cameras or memory cards.

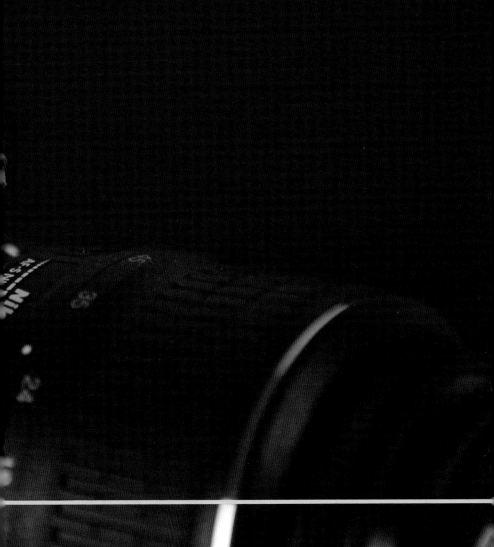

Chapter 9
CONNECTION

9 CONNECTION

In digital photography, connecting to external devices—especially computers—is not an optional extra: it's how you store, organize, backup and print images. The D3200 is designed to facilitate these operations, and the main cables required are included with the camera.

» CONNECTING TO A COMPUTER

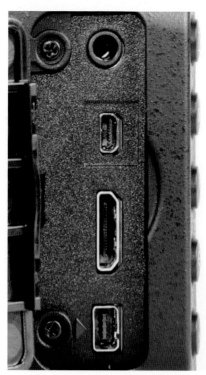

Connecting to a Mac or PC allows you to store and backup your images. It also helps you exploit more of the power of the D3200, including the ability to optimize image quality from RAW files. The supplied Nikon Transfer software allows you to control this process, while Nikon View NX2 has a range of image enhancement tools. Nikon Capture NX2 (extra) has greater capabilities, especially when working with RAW files. The optional Nikon Camera

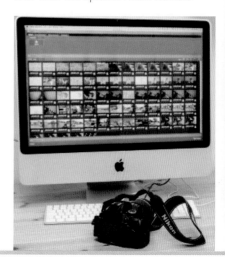

Connection ports on the left side of the D3200 ☆

A D3200 connected to a computer »

Note:
The supplied USB cable allows direct connection to a computer. However, it's often more convenient to transfer photos by inserting the memory card into a card-reader. Many PCs have built-in SD card slots but separate card-readers are cheap and widely available. Older card-readers may not support SDHC or SDXC cards.

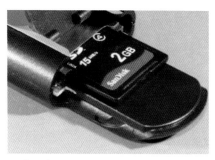

Card-reader

Control Pro 2 software allows camera operation to be controlled directly from the Mac or PC. There are third-party alternatives to all of these apps.

software, but such systems may run very slowly when dealing with the large image files produced by the D3200, and may have particular difficulty in opening RAW files.

› Computer requirements

Most modern computers are more than capable. You'll need a USB port for connecting the camera (or card-reader), unless you connect wirelessly using an Eye-Fi card *(see page 235)*. You can install Nikon software from the supplied CD or download it from the Nikon website.

Nikon Transfer and Nikon View NX2 require one of the following operating systems:

Mac OS X (Version 10.5.68 or later); Windows 7 (Service Pack 1); Windows Vista (Service Pack 2); Windows XP (32-bit) with Service Pack 3. Mac OS 9 and earlier versions of Windows are not supported.

Older computers will still be able to transfer and view images using third-party

› Backing up

Until they are backed up, your precious images exist solely as data on the camera's memory card. Memory cards are robust but not indestructible, and in any case you will surely wish to format and reuse them. However, when images are transferred to

Tip

If your computer runs slowly when working with large image files, the most likely cause is insufficient memory (RAM). RAM can usually be added relatively cheaply and easily. A shortage of free space on the hard disk may also cause a slowdown.

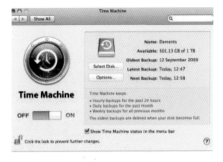

Apple's Time Machine maintains backups automatically ««

This is the Display Calibrator Assistant included in Mac OS X ❯❯

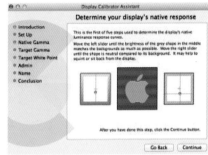

the computer and the card is formatted, those images still exist in one single location, the computer's hard drive. If anything happens to that hard drive, whether fire, theft or hardware failure, you could lose thousands of irreplaceable images. The simplest form of backup is to a second hard drive.

› Color calibration

A major headache for digital camera users is that images look one way on the camera monitor, different on the computer screen, different when you email them to your friends, and different again when printed. To achieve consistency across different devices, it's vital above all that your main computer screen is correctly set up and calibrated. This may seem complex and time-consuming but ultimately saves much time and frustration. Detailed advice is beyond the scope of this book but try searching System Help for "monitor calibration". There's more detail in the

Digital SLR Handbook (from this author and publisher) and there's some useful advice at http://www.cambridgeincolour.com/color-management-printing.htm.

› Connecting the camera

This description is based on Nikon Transfer, part of the supplied View NX2 package— and assumes you have already installed this. The procedure with other software will be similar in outline but different in detail.

1) Turn the computer on and allow it to start up fully. Open the cover on the left side of the camera and insert the smaller end of the supplied USB cable into the USB slot; insert the other end into a USB port on the computer (don't try connecting to unpowered USB hubs or

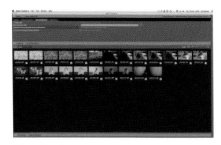

Nikon Transfer

ports on the keyboard; they won't work).

2) Turn the camera ON. Nikon Transfer starts automatically (unless you have configured its Preferences otherwise), and a window like the one illustrated appears on the computer screen.

3) The Nikon Transfer window offers various options; for full detail see the Help menu in Nikon Transfer itself. The following are among the most important.

4) To transfer selected images only, use the check box below each thumbnail to select/deselect as required.

5) Click the **Primary Destination** tab to choose where photos will be stored. You can create a new subfolder for each transfer, rename images as they are transferred, and so on.

6) Click the **Backup Destination** tab if you want Nikon Transfer to create backup copies automatically during transfer.

› Disconnecting the camera

Simply switch OFF the camera when transfer is complete, and disconnect the cable. Nikon Transfer will close automatically. If you transfer images using a card-reader, you must remove the card from the system like any other external drive. For instance, in Windows XP or Vista, use Safely Remove Hardware; in Mac OS X use Command + E or drag the D3200 icon to the Trash.

› Wireless connection (Eye-Fi)

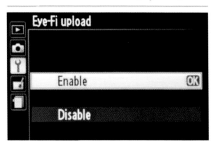

Eye-Fi upload item in the Setup menu

An Eye-Fi card looks and operates like a conventional (albeit more expensive) SD memory card, but includes an antenna which enables it to connect to WiFi networks, allowing speedy transfer of images to a computer without cables.

Eye-Fi cards are supplied with a card reader. When the card and reader are plugged into any recent Mac or PC the supplied software should install automatically. (Of course the computer must also have a Wi-Fi connection.) There's then an automatic registration process which makes that computer the default destination for Eye-Fi upload. You can select a destination folder on your computer and you can also configure the system to automatically upload photos to sharing sites such as Flickr.

Once configuration is complete, insert the card in the camera. Use the **Eye-Fi upload** item in the Setup menu and then the camera will automatically upload images as they are taken, as long as you remain within signal range of the network. The D3200 displays a notification when images are being uploaded.

Warning!

On most WiFi networks, uploading can be quite a slow process. It can certainly lag far behind the speed at which you can shoot images. Don't switch off the camera until images have finished uploading, although upload should resume when you turn it on again. Uploading by Eye-Fi is a drain on the battery. Even when beyond network range, the card will transmit in an attempt to connect. To preserve battery life, disable Eye-Fi upload when not using it.

» NIKON SOFTWARE

The D3200 is bundled with Nikon View NX2 software. This includes Nikon Transfer, a simple application that does a simple job competently. Nikon View NX2 itself covers most of the main processes in digital photography: you can view and browse images, save them in other formats, and print. Though View NX2 is much better than View NX, editing and enhancing images (including RAW files) is still slow and not very intuitive, comparing poorly with apps like iPhoto. Results might be technically superior, but getting there might try your patience. It's also weak when it comes to organizing/cataloging.

Nikon Capture NX2 has much wider functionality but still feels awkward beside mainstream applications like Adobe Photoshop. Capture NX2 is not included with the camera and you will have to pay to download it or obtain it on CD.

› Using Nikon View NX2

1) From a browser view such as the thumbnail grid (choose view mode from the **View** menu), click on an image to highlight it. **Image Viewer** shows the image in more detail, plus a histogram, and **Full Screen** allows you to see the image full size.

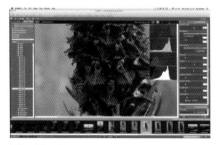
Nikon View NX2

2) Panels on the right side of the screen reveal **Metadata** (detailed info about the image), and the **Adjustment** palette, which allows a range of adjustments such as exposure and white balance. It also has access to Nikon Picture Controls *(see page 87)*.

3) Any adjustments you make will be recorded automatically. You do not need to export or convert the file immediately.

4) To export the file as a TIFF or JPEG which can be viewed, edited and printed by most other applications, choose **Convert Files** from the **File** menu. Here you can set a new size for the image if required, and also change its name.

5) The **File Format** drop-down menu in the **Convert Files** dialog offers three options: **JPEG**, **TIFF(8 Bit)**, **TIFF(16 Bit)**.

› Nikon Capture NX2

Nikon Capture NX2 is a far more complete editing package than Nikon View. For access to a full range of editing options, especially in relation to RAW files, Nikon Capture NX2 (or one of its third-party rivals) is essential. However, if you use, or have legacy photos from, any non-Nikon cameras, Capture NX2 cannot open RAW files from these. Photoshop has a much wider feature set, but is typically around four times dearer. If you already own an

Nikon View NX2 file format options

JPEG	Choose compression ratio: Highest Quality; High Quality; Good Balance; Good Compression Ratio; Highest Compression Ratio.	Suitable if extensive further editing is not envisaged. It's recommended to choose Highest Quality unless storage space is at a premium, or the image is specifically intended for such use as an email attachment.
TIFF (8-bit)		Creates larger file sizes than JPEG, but is a better choice if subsequent editing is envisaged; however, 16-bit is advised for extensive retouching work.
TIFF (16-bit)		The best choice when further editing is anticipated. Images can be converted to 8-bit after editing, halving file size.

9

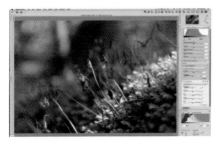

Nikon Capture NX2

older version of Photoshop, upgrades may be much cheaper, while many will find that alternatives like Lightroom, Aperture or Photoshop Elements (see below) will meet all their needs.

Capture NX2 is not included with the camera and you will have to pay to download it or obtain it on CD.

» THIRD-PARTY SOFTWARE

The undisputed monarch of image-editing software is Adobe Photoshop, the current version being Photoshop CS6. Its power is

enormous and it's the subject of many dedicated books and websites. It also costs significantly more than a D3200 body. (If you already own an older version of Photoshop, upgrades are cheaper.)

It is far more than many users need, and many will prefer Photoshop Elements, at a tenth of the price, which still has sophisticated editing features, including the ability to open RAW files from the D3200.

Photoshop Elements also includes something that Adobe Photoshop itself does not, namely its Organizer module, which allows photos to be sorted into "Albums" and also "tagged" in different ways. Some sort of organizer or cataloging software becomes essential as you amass hundreds and then thousands of images.

Mac users have another excellent choice in the form of iPhoto (latest version iPhoto 11), pre-loaded on new Macs; like Photoshop Elements, it combines organizing and editing abilities.

PHOTOSHOP ELEMENTS ✖
Adobe Photoshop Elements: Organizer module.

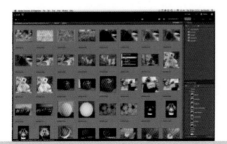

iPHOTO ✖
iPhoto's Adjust options.

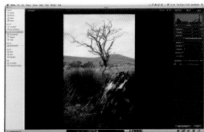

There's no easier imaging software to grasp, and the Adjust palette provides quick and flexible image editing too. iPhoto can open RAW files from the D3200, but—unlike Photoshop Elements—cannot edit in 16-bit depth, which is recommended for best results.

Finally, if you regularly shoot RAW, there are one-stop solutions in the shape of Apple's Aperture (Mac only) and Adobe Lightroom (Mac and PC). Both applications combine powerful organizing and cataloging with sophisticated and non-destructive image editing. Essentially this means that edit settings (any changes you make to your image, including color, density, cropping and so on) are recorded alongside the original RAW file without any need to create a new TIFF or JPEG file. TIFF or JPEG versions, incorporating all the edits, can be exported as and when needed.

ADOBE LIGHTROOM ⹊
Adobe Lightroom's Develop module offers a very wide spectrum of RAW adjustments.

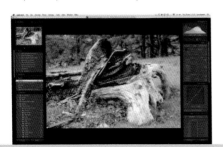

» CONNECTING TO A TV

The supplied EG-CP14 cable is used to connect the camera to a normal TV or VCR. You can also connect the camera to an HDMI (High Definition Multimedia Interface) TV but you'll need an HDMI cable (not supplied). In other respects the process is the same.

1) Check that the camera is set to the correct mode in the Setup menu (NTSC or PAL for standard TVs and VCRs or HDMI).

2) Turn the camera OFF (always do this before connecting or disconnecting the cable).

3) Open the cover on the left side of the camera and insert the cable into the appropriate slot (A/V-out or HDMI).

4) Tune the TV to the Video or HDMI channel.

5) Turn the camera ON and press the playback button. Images remain visible on the camera monitor as well as on the TV and you navigate using the Multi-selector in the usual way. The D3200's Slide show facility *(see Playback menu, page 94)* can be used to automate playback.

The most flexible and powerful way to print photographs from the D3200 is to transfer them to a computer. This is the only option where RAW files are concerned (though you can always create JPEG copies, *see page 111).*

The memory card can also be inserted into a compatible printer or taken to a photo printing store. Finally, the camera can be connected to any printer that supports the PictBridge standard, allowing JPEG images to be printed directly.

› To connect to a printer

1) Turn the camera OFF.

2) Turn the printer on and connect the supplied USB cable. Open the cover on the left side of the camera and insert the cable into the USB slot; the smaller end of the cable connects to the camera.

3) Turn the camera ON. You should now see a welcome screen, followed by a PictBridge playback display. There's now a choice between **Printing pictures one at a time** or **Printing multiple pictures**.

› Printing pictures one at a time

This process is very straightforward, particularly if you are already familiar with navigating the D3200's playback screens.

1) Press ▶. If the photo which appears is the one you wish to print, press **OK**. If not, navigate to the required photo in the usual way *(see page 82)* and then press **OK**.

2) This brings up a menu of printing options (see table opposite). Use the Multi-selector to navigate through the menu and highlight specific options. Press **OK** to select the highlighted option.

3) When the required options have been set, select **Start printing** and press **OK**. To cancel at any time, press **OK** again.

Printing options

Option name	Options available	Notes
Page size	Printer default	Options will be limited by the maximum size the printer can print.
	3.5 x 5in	
	5 x 7in	
	A4	
No of copies	1–99	Use ▲ / ▼ to choose number, then press **OK** to select.
Border	Printer default	If **Print with border** is selected, borders will be white.
	Print with border	
	No border	
Time stamp	Printer default	Prints time and date when image was taken.
	Print time stamp	
	No time stamp	
Crop	Crop	Prints selected area only to size selected under **Page size**.
	No cropping	

› Image cropping

If **Crop** is selected, the image is displayed again with a border delineating the crop area. Use the ⊖✕ and ⊕ buttons to change the size of the crop area and use the Multi-selector to reposition it if you don't want it centered. (This is all very similar to using **Trim** in the Retouch Menu, *see page 109*.) When satisfied, press **OK** and continue to **Start printing**.

› Printing multiple pictures

You can print several pictures at once. You can also create an index print of all JPEG images (up to a maximum of 256) currently stored on the memory card.

If the PictBridge menu is not already displayed, press **MENU**. The options in the following table are displayed:

Print Select	Use the Multi-selector to scroll through pictures on the memory card (displayed as six thumbnails at a time). To see an image full screen, press ⊕🔲. To choose the currently selected image for printing, hold ⊡ and press ▲. The picture is marked with a **PRINT** and the number of prints set to 1. Keep ⊕🔲 depressed and use ▲ to change the number of prints.
	Repeat the above to select further images and choose the number of prints required from each. Finally, press **OK** to display the PictBridge menu and select printing options, as in the table *on page 241*.
	Only the options for **Page size**, **Border**, and **Time stamp** will be available.
	Select **Start printing** and press **OK**.
Select date	Prints one copy of each image taken on a selected date.
Print (DPOF)	Prints images already selected using the **Print set (DPOF)** option in the Playback menu *(see page 95)*.
Index Print	Prints all JPEG images (up to a maximum of 256) on the memory card. If more than 256 images exist, only the first 256 will be printed. Options for **Page size**, **Border**, and **Time stamp** can be set as already described. If the selected page size is too small for the number of images, a warning will be displayed.

8-bit, **12-bit**, **16-bit**: *see* bit depth.

Accessory shoe *see* hotshoe.

Aperture The lens opening which admits light. Relative aperture sizes are expressed in f-numbers (*see* below).

Artefact Occurs when data or data produced by the sensor is interpreted incorrectly, resulting in visible flaws in the image.

Bit depth The amount of information recorded for each color channel. 8-bit, for example, means that the data distinguishes 2^8 or 256 levels of brightness for each channel. 16-bit images recognize over 65,000 levels per channel, which allows greater freedom in editing. The D3200 records RAW images in 12-bit depth and they are converted to 16-bit on import to the computer.

Bracketing Taking a number of otherwise identical shots in which just one parameter (e.g. exposure) is varied.

Buffer On-board memory that holds images until they can be written to the memory card.

Burst A number of frames shot in quick succession; the maximum burst size is limited by buffer capacity.

Channel The D3200, like other digital devices, records data for three separate color channels (*see* RGB).

CCD (charge-coupled device) A type of image sensor used in many digital cameras.

Clipping Complete loss of detail in highlight or shadow areas of the image (sometimes both!), leaving them as blank white or black.

CMOS (complementary metal oxide semiconductor) A type of image sensor used in many digital cameras, including the D3200.

Color temperature The color of light, expressed in degrees Kelvin (K). Confusingly, "cool" (bluer) light has a higher color temperature than "warm" (red) light.

CPU (central processing unit) Really a small computer in the camera (also found in many lenses) that controls most or all of the unit's functions.

Crop factor *see* focal length multiplication factor.

Diopter Unit expressing the power of a lens.

dpi (dots per inch) A measure of resolution; should strictly be applied only to printers (*see* ppi).

Dynamic range The range of brightness from shadows to highlights within which the camera can record detail.

Exposure Used in several senses. For instance, "an exposure" is virtually synonymous with "an image" or "a photo": to make an exposure = to take a picture. Exposure also refers to the amount of light hitting the image sensor, and to systems of measuring this. *See* also overexposure, underexposure.

Ev (exposure value) A standardized unit of exposure. 1 Ev is equivalent to 1 "stop" in traditional photographic parlance.

Extension rings/Extension tubes Hollow tubes which fit between the camera tube and lens, used to allow greater magnifications.

f-number Lens aperture expressed as a fraction of focal length—f/2 is a wide aperture and f/16 is narrow.

Fast (lens) Lens with a wide maximum aperture, e.g. f1.8. f/4 might be considered relatively fast for long telephotos.

Fill-in flash Flash used in combination with daylight. Used with naturally backlit or harshly side-lit subjects to prevent dark shadows.

Filter A piece of glass or plastic placed in front of, within, or behind the lens to modify light.

Firmware Software which controls the camera: upgrades are issued by Nikon from time to time and can be transferred to the camera via a memory card.

Focal length The distance (in mm) from the optical center of a lens to the point at which light is focused.

Focal length multiplication factor Because the D3200's sensor is smaller than a frame of 35mm film, the effective focal length of all lenses is multiplied by 1.5.

fps (frames per second) The number of exposures (photographs) that can be taken in a second. The D3200's maximum rate is 4fps.

Highlights The brightest areas of the scene and/or the image.

Histogram A graph representing the distribution of tones in an image, ranging from pure black to pure white.

Incident light metering Measuring the light falling on to a subject, usually with a separate meter. An alternative to the in-camera meter, which measures reflected light.

ISO (International Standards Organization) ISO ratings express film speed. Strictly speaking, the sensitivity of digital sensors should be quoted as "ISO-equivalent".

JPEG (from Joint Photographic Experts Group) A compressed image file standard. High levels of JPEG compression can reduce files to about 5% of their original size, but there may be some loss of quality.

LCD (liquid crystal display) Flat screen like the D3200's rear monitor.

Macro A term used to describe close focusing and close-focusing ability of a lens. A true macro lens has a reproduction ratio of 1:1 or better.

Megapixel see pixel.

Memory card A removable storage device for digital cameras.

Noise Image interference manifested as random variations in pixel brightness and/or color.

Overexposure When too much light reaches the sensor, resulting in a too-bright image, often with clipped highlights.

Pixel Picture element; the individual colored dots (usually square) which make up a digital image. One million pixels = 1 megapixel.

ppi (pixels per inch) Should be applied to digital files rather than the commonly used dpi.

Reproduction ratio The ratio between the real size of an object and the size of its image on the sensor.

Resolution The number of pixels for a given dimension, for example 300 pixels per inch. Resolution is often confused with image size. The native size of an image from the D3200 is 4608 x 3072 pixels. This could make a large but coarse print at 100 dpi or a smaller but finer one at 300 dpi.

RGB (red, green, blue) Digital devices, including the D3200, record color in terms of brightness levels of the three primary colors.

Sensor The light-sensitive chip at the heart of every digital camera.

Shutter The mechanism which controls the amount of light reaching the sensor by opening and closing to expose the sensor when the shutter-release button is pushed.

Speedlight Nikon's range of dedicated external flashguns.

Spot metering A metering system which takes its reading from the light reflected by a small portion of the scene.

Telephoto (lens) A lens with a large focal length and a narrow angle of view.

TIFF (Tagged Image File Format) A universal file format supported by virtually all image-editing applications.

TTL (through the lens) The viewing and metering of SLR cameras such as the D3200.

Underexposure When insufficient light reaches the sensor, resulting in a too-dark image, often with clipped shadows.

USB (Universal Serial Bus) A data transfer standard, used to connect to a computer.

Viewfinder An optical system used for framing the image. On an SLR camera like the D3200 the viewfinder shows the view as seen through the lens.

White balance A function which compensates for different color temperatures so that images may be recorded with correct color balance.

Wide-angle (lens) A lens with a short focal length and a wide angle of view.

Zoom (lens) A lens with variable focal length, giving a range of viewing angles. To zoom in is to change focal length to give a narrower view and zoom out is the converse. Optical zoom refers to the genuine zoom ability of a lens; digital zoom is the cropping of part of an image to produce an illusion of the same effect.

9 » USEFUL WEB SITES

NIKON-RELATED SITES

Nikon Worldwide
Home page for the Nikon Corporation
www.nikon.com

Nikon USA
Home page for Nikon USA
www.nikonusa.com

Nikon UK
Home page for Nikon UK
www.nikon.co.uk

Nikon User Support
www.nikonusa.com/Service-And-Support/
www.europe-nikon.com/support

Nikon Historical Society
Worldwide site for study of Nikon products
www.nikonhs.org

Nikon Links
Links to many Nikon-related sites
www.nikonlinks.com

Grays of Westminster
Revered Nikon-only London dealer
www.graysofwestminster.co.uk

GENERAL SITES

Digital Photography Review
Independent news and reviews
www.dpreview.com

Thom Hogan
Real-world reviews and advice
www.bythom.com/nikon.htm

Jon Sparks
Landscape and outdoor pursuits
photography
www.jon-sparks.co.uk

EQUIPMENT AND SOFTWARE

Adobe
Photoshop, Photoshop Elements, Lightroom
www.adobe.com/uk

Apple
Aperture and iPhoto
www.apple.com/uk/mac/

Aquapac
Waterproof cases
www.aquapac.net

Think Tank Photo
(Bags, holsters, rain-covers)
www.thinktankphoto.com

Sigma
Independent lenses and flash units
www.sigmaphoto.com
www.sigma-imaging-uk.com

PHOTOGRAPHY PUBLICATIONS

Ammonite Press
Photography books
www.ammonitepress.com

***Black & White Photography* magazine,
Outdoor Photography magazine**
www.thegmcgroup.com

» INDEX